LNER IN TRANSITION
Michael Blakemore

CONTENTS

Blue-liveried A4 No.60015 Quicksilver *hurries north from Potters Bar on Sunday 10th September 1950 with the down 3.00pm from King's Cross to Newcastle conveying through coaches to Tyne Commission Quay (at North Shields) for the Bergen Line night sailing to Norway. No.60015 was still a Grantham engine at this time but the following year it was decided to congregate all the Eastern Region's A4s at King's Cross as part of a major campaign to improve motive power reliability on the ECML.* (Eric Bruton)

INTRODUCTION

The railways of Britain have only lately come through the huge organisational transition from public to private ownership, but 55 years ago there was the major upheaval during which the 'Big Four' companies were taken into State control as British Railways. As in all such transitions the railways underwent a radical visual change over a period of some years as the new styles and practices of British Railways gradually eliminated old identities.

LNER in Transition is the theme of this book and it is presented as a pictorial record of the railway and its successor from the close of the company era to about 1952 by which time its name and style had been largely (but not yet entirely) erased. There is, admittedly, nothing of particular historical significance in this period, but it was visually interesting as years of change often are — the last chance to see familiar engines in famous old liveries, the dawning realisation that a new publicly-owned age had begun as the words 'BRITISH RAILWAYS' were paraded on tenders or tank sides, the first sightings of new locomotives commissioned in the dying days of the former company.

Those who enjoy following the ever-evolving appearance of the railways will hopefully enjoy this glimpse of an intriguing and short-lived period. Modellers, too, may find inspiration; the LNER and BR periods both have their devotees but the transitional years have perhaps not attracted the same attention in modelling circles even though they offer a range of contrasting possibilities.

The opportunity to compile this selection was principally suggested by a fine collection of photographs presented some years ago to Pendragon by the late Eric Bruton. Eric made a tentative start in railway photography in 1932 using a box camera bought by his father with the aid of cigarette coupons. In due course he took up photography as a serious hobby and was a member of the Railway Photographic Society from 1947. A draughtsman by profession, Eric was to become a photographer of exceptional skill and his collection of negatives is now in the care of the National Railway Museum. Living not far from the East Coast Main Line in Hertfordshire, he was perfectly placed to record the transitional scene near his home and also on his travels. To him, and all those others whose enjoyment of photographing trains and railways has left us with such a rich pictorial legacy, we owe our thanks.

Michael Blakemore
York, August 2003

King's Cross for the North. Lewis Cubitt's simple yet elegant terminus stands on the Euston Road against the background of a battle-scarred London in this view on 11th August 1952. The tower contains Frederick Dent's clock displayed at the 1851 Great Exhibition. The front of the station is marred, however, by the untidy jumble of shacks which sprang up and came to be known as the 'African village'. King's Cross did not escape the war unscathed and an air raid in May 1941 saw part of the roof destroyed, along with the booking hall. During its final year the LNER restored the roof, then BR added its name to the façade but nothing was done to clear away the shabby clutter in front of the station for another quarter of a century.
(Pendragon collection)

EAST SIDE STORY

The railways seem always to have been in transition. The London & North Eastern Railway was a product of a major piece of organisational upheaval, the Railways Act of 1921, which brought it and the others of the so-called 'Big Four' (London Midland & Scottish Railway, Great Western Railway and Southern Railway) into being. Over the years before that, an on-going series of takeovers and amalgamations had seen the eventual establishment of the 'heavyweight' companies which existed at the time of the enforced grouping of 1923.

The Great Northern Railway operated the main line from London to Doncaster and associated secondary routes, while in East Anglia the Great Eastern was virtually unchallenged. The powerful North Eastern Railway ran a monopolistic fiefdom in the area suggested by its title, encompassing much of the North and East Ridings of Yorkshire but also, significantly, the heavily-industrialised area of Durham and Northumberland; only in the south east of its domain had the Hull & Barnsley Railway tweaked its tail, but the two had already combined in 1922. The NER also held the East Coast Main Line until at Berwick it met the North British Railway, a forceful player in the Scottish scene whose network continued the main line on to Edinburgh and Aberdeen and crossed from Edinburgh to Glasgow, then out via the spectacular West Highland line to the west coast at Mallaig. In the farthest north east of the land the Great North of Scotland ran a tight though impoverished operation whose efficiency, by the turn of the century, had banished an earlier lamentable reputation.

Collectively they were a hotch-potch but adding to the eventual LNER family was a pushy upstart called the Manchester, Sheffield & Lincolnshire Railway which took it upon itself to extend its local operations and to achieve its ambition of creating a new route to London. Having done so, it restyled itself the Great Central Railway in 1897 and became operator of the 'Last Main Line' and of the capital's newest terminus, Marylebone, but remained as the most controversial of the LNER's constituents. In building Marylebone the railway had allowed for the expansion of the station and the increase in the number of platforms which the growth of traffic was expected to demand; it never did and Marylebone, half-completed with just four platforms, remained the capital's smallest and quietest terminus.

It was Government legislation which created the LNER and Government legislation which brought its 25 years' existence to an end, when the Transport Act 1947 established the nationalised British Railways on the following 1st January. But if a quarter of a century is not, in the scheme of things, a very long life, the LNER certainly packed a lot into it and during the late 1920s/1930s it repeatedly hit the headlines: a London—Newcastle non-stop service, then the London to Edinburgh non-stop, the introduction of the streamlined locomotives and the various streamlined train services, a succession of speed records culminating in *Mallard's* world record. An imaginative publicity department kept the LNER in the public eye and maintained its reputation for flair and excitement.

Yet for all its pizzazz, the LNER was always the weakest, financially, of the Big Four. Although it served the mining areas of the east Midlands, Yorkshire and the north east, the steelworks of north east Lincolnshire and the fishing, shipbuilding, trading and ferry ports along the east coast, these traditional industries were badly hit by the recessions of the 1920s and '30s, seriously affecting the company's revenue, most of which was derived from freight traffic. At the same time, although it operated the important East Coast Main Line, much of the LNER's network lay in sparsely-populated regions — East Anglia, the North and East Ridings of Yorkshire, the Scottish borders and the north east of Scotland — where passenger numbers were always going to be modest.

The Railways Act had provided for the Big Four to earn a 'standard revenue' (based on 1913 figures), yet it was a largely unworkable formula given the changes occurring during the 1920s due to economic fluctuations and the sort of transport competition to which railways had not hitherto been exposed. The LNER never managed to achieve its standard revenue and struggled financially throughout its existence; its shareholders were invariably disappointed by their returns. Not that the LNER was alone in facing difficult times; along with the other companies it twice enforced temporary wage cuts, a remedy unimaginable today.

For all that, many still look at the sixteen years between 1923 and 1939 as an epic period but even if that were so, it was an exciting era brought abruptly to an end by the outbreak of World War II. The years between 1939 and 1945 saw the railways play a heroic role in the national war effort, but at a cost. The LNER was faced with hauling heavy trainloads of armaments and munitions, troops, evacuees, fuel and civilians — everything and everyone. It had to contend with bombing raids as the enemy attacked London and major industrial and

The 8.24am Grantham—King's Cross is seen south of Hatfield on 16th April 1949 headed by A3 4-6-2 No.60096 Papyrus which is in a combination of LNER apple green livery and British Railways number and markings. Behind the locomotive is a three-lavatory articulated twin set, a type built for outer suburban use, which had probably been added to strengthen the train due to overcrowding. Such service...! (Eric Bruton)

commercial centres like Sheffield, Hull and Newcastle, all of which took their toll on railway installations; then came the so-called 'Baedeker Raids' (named after the famous guidebooks to historic cities) on York and Norwich. Later the railway had to contend with the V1 flying bombs (the 'doodlebugs') and V2 rockets; the first of the V1s to land in Britain came down on the LNER between Bethnal Green and Stratford. By the time peace returned, all this, and the minimal maintenance possible just to keep things going, had left the LNER in a severely rundown condition.

During the war the railways had been under Government control and the agreement enforcing that had provided for them to be financially compensated by rentals calculated on a basis of the average net revenues for 1935/6/7. The LNER should therefore have received a 23% share of a £39.4 million total. Furthermore, the railways should have been able to retain revenues up to £43.5 million; anything between that and £56 million would be shared between railways and State, while any revenue in excess of the latter sum was kept by the State. However, the Government scrapped this agreement in 1941, fixed the maximum rental at £43 million and took *all* the excess revenue above that. Since the railways' income increased by 154% between 1939 and 1944 due to the volume of wartime traffic, they were in effect short-changed by the Government; thus it was that the LNER (like the rest) reached the post-war period in a poor financial (even by its standards!) as well as physical state.

The election in 1945 of a Labour government committed to a policy of public ownership meant that the writing was on the wall for the LNER and the Transport Bill came before Parliament in November 1946. This book is not the place to argue the case for or against nationalization or to describe the process by which it happened, except to say that the LNER was opposed to it on principle and campaigned vigorously against it. In 1946 it published a paper entitled *The State and the Railways — An Alternative to Nationalisation* but it was swimming against the political tide.

Despite a somewhat unreal couple of years carrying on business as usual while awaiting the inevitable, the LNER *did* to some extent move forward. For example, it acted to dispel some of the wartime drabness by reinstating its colourful locomotive liveries — apple green on express passenger and some mixed traffic engines, garter blue again for the A4 streamliners. Then at the beginning of 1946 it embarked on a complete renumbering of its locomotive fleet, a scheme first drawn up in 1943. This gave consecutive blocks of numbers to particular locomotive classes, a considerable improvement on the previous haphazard numbering arrangement; the task was completed in little over a year.

The nationalised British Railways came into existence on 1st January 1948 and a good many of the LNER's senior officers took up important management posts within the new State undertaking. a telling testimony to their undoubted skills. In the event, the administration of the post-nationalisation

Gresley's famous Pacifics dominated the East Coast Main Line throughout the LNER era until the demise of steam under British Railways, but new designs were put into service by his successors Edward Thompson and Arthur Peppercorn. Thompson had introduced a new standard 4-6-2 (later designated Class A2/3) but following his retirement in 1946 Peppercorn produced an improved design of which just the first had been built by the time nationalisation arrived. The remaining thirteen of the class were completed by BR, including No. 60534 **Irish Elegance.** *The locomotive was just two months old when photographed at York shed on 12th June 1948 being coaled by crane and skip, presumably due to a breakdown of the mechanical coaling plant. All the Peppercorn A2s were turned out in LNER green livery but from the outset No. 60534 had 'British Railways' markings and number and a smokebox numberplate. Its name perpetuates the LNER's racehorse naming tradition.* (J.W. Hague/D.V. Beeken collection)

railway was a complex affair, an often unwieldy combination of central control and regionalism drawing on company heritage; unfortunately the pre-1948 companies had largely stood back from advising on a more suitable construction. The railways were vested in the British Transport Commission which, it was envisaged, would co-ordinate all its various elements (including road haulage, waterways and docks) in a vision of an integrated State-owned transport system. 'Integrated public transport' is a concept which has been depicted from time to time as a sort of 'Holy Grail' to be aimed at, but it was no more achieved then than now! Management of the railways was devolved to The Railway Executive to which members were appointed by the Minister of Transport and which established for itself a measure of independence; 'British Railways' was its trading name. It saw as one of its most important objectives the return of the railway network to the sort of standards which had existed pre-war and regarded 'integration' as not really its main concern.

For most practical purposes the railways were divided into six Regions and it was in their defined boundaries (in England anyway) that, in spite of the general principle of unifying the former privately-owned system, company influences and

J72 0-6-0T No.8680 was painted in full LNER green livery in May 1947 for its role as station pilot at Newcastle Central. This North Eastern Railway design dated from 1898 but remarkably the class was by no means complete when this photograph was taken. In 1943 Thompson had drawn up a locomotive standardisation plan for future development in which the Great Northern J50 type was identified as the standard heavy shunting tank but in 1946 Peppercorn sub-stituted the J72 and ordered a further batch. These were deferred until 1949 and it was BR which between then and 1951 added 28 more. (J.W. Hague/D.V. Beeken collection)

practices lived on. As far as the LNER was concerned, the vast majority of its route mileage ended up distributed over three of these BR Regions.

Virtually all the old Great Northern, Great Eastern and Great Central systems went into the Eastern Region which had its offices at Liverpool Street in what had been the home of the LNER Southern Area. This Region would have held sway up to the Scottish border were it not for a late decision to create a separate North Eastern Region with headquarters in York. The LNER had based its North Eastern Area there and before that it had, of course, been the centre of the old North Eastern

6

The LNER had not been able or, indeed, inclined to pursue the sort of 'scrap and build' policy favoured by the LMS and so British Railways inherited quite a substantial fleet of locomotives from the LNER's pre-grouping constituents. Outside Kittybrewster shed, Aberdeen, on 4th June 1950 is D40 4-4-0 No.62272 which had been built by the Great North of Scotland Railway in 1910. It has gained the lined black livery decided upon for mixed traffic locomotives but not yet the first BR emblem on its tender.
(Pendragon collection)

Railway. Although across the country the London Midland Region extended all the way from London to the Scottish border, there had been thoughts in the planning of the Regional system of a 'North Western Region' but such was the complexity of the network that it would have been quite difficult to define workable boundaries; the identifying of a North Eastern Region, with just the one main line running north—south and secondary routes branching off it, was much simpler. A new Scottish Region embraced all the lines of both the LNER and the LMSR north of the border. Curiously, the

idea of a Scottish company had been one of the Government's preferred options back at the time that the Grouping was being discussed before the 1921 Railways Act; equally curiously, given today's devolutionary climate, the Scottish railways were opposed, fearing their financial weakness as against the more prosperous companies coming up from England, and got their way.

It can therefore be seen that in many practical ways the territorial organisation of the railways was maintained after nationalisation and old company boundaries could clearly be identified in its structure. Perhaps this was a good thing since it ensured continuity to quite a considerable extent, with many people remaining to do much the same jobs as they had done before in the same offices — and also ensured that the influence of the 'Big Four' endured long beyond its actual lifespan. The concept of a major railway upheaval which concluded with a continuity of function and an experienced workforce to do it has eluded the responsible authorities pretty well ever since 1947!

Notions of remote bodies like the BTC and the RE were largely irrelevant to passengers and probably to employees (apart from in matters of pay). Users of the LNER became users of the Eastern, North Eastern and Scottish Regions of BR and eventually came to identify these as the outfits which operated their stations, issued their timetables and ran their trains. In everyday terms, to the average railway user nationalisation brought little real change, except that bit by bit the railway began to look different. It made no difference to the ease of long journeys involving two or more pre-1948 railways since the old companies had long-established through ticketing arrangements, the finances of which were later efficiently sorted out by the clerks of the Railway Clearing House — modern train operators please note!

It would be more in the 'looking different' area that people would have noted that a transition was under way, during which the LNER's visible legacy lingered but gradually disappeared. Its livery remained on its locomotives for a while but acquired the name and numbers of the new ownership until BR decided on and applied colour schemes of its own. After trialling a range of experimental liveries, BR settled on a rich blue with black and white lining (similar to that of the old Caledonian Railway) for the principal express classes, green lined in orange and black for other main passenger types, LNWR-style lined black for mixed traffic types and plain black for the rest. The blue was found not to wear well in traffic and was soon discarded in favour of the green. At the same time the BTC concocted a form of 'logo' which could be widely used and this appeared in the form of a somewhat scrawny lion astride a wheel, soon acquiring the scathing nickname 'ferret and dartboard' amongst enthusiasts; the device was applied to locomotives to supplant use of the words 'BRITISH RAILWAYS'. The last of the LNER's locomotives did not depart the stage until 1967, the final full year of steam on British Railways.

The LNER's varnished teak coaching stock, a finish going back to the Great Northern and the East Coast Joint Stock, and

the 'mock teak' of Edward Thompson's later steel-panelled vehicles gave way to something far more garish as BR repainted its acquired main line carriages in a crimson and cream livery and its local stock in all-over crimson. The last of the LNER's teak-bodied buffet cars remained in traffic well into 1970s, by then in BR's *third* livery of blue and grey.

Stations and signs, too, gained a new look but here the Regional individualism provided its own variety as each was allotted its own colour. The Eastern Region had dark blue, which had its origins in LNER usage, while the Scottish Region used a lighter blue which, it is supposed, drew its inspiration from the Caledonian colour. The North Eastern Region had tangerine, which had (as far as I can see) no obvious heritage. Many existing signs were simply repainted but over time new enamel signs were installed, the most distinctive being the RE's 'totem' (which is regarded as having its ancestry in London Transport's famous bar and circle) carrying station names against the Regional colour background.

In the very first month of the nationalised era former-Great Eastern J69 0-6-0T No. 8619 was chosen to act as station pilot at Liverpool Street and Stratford Works turned it out in fully-lined LNER green livery though with 'BRITISH RAILWAYS' lettering and an 'E' prefix to its number denoting an Eastern Region allocation as a preliminary to the full renumbering of all LNER locomotives by adding 60000 to their post-1946 numbers. As is evident, it was maintained in immaculate condition by its crews. (Pendragon collection)

As I write, 56 years have gone by since the LNER officially passed out of existence, so what remains to remind us of it? In terms of LNER locomotives in preservation, there are disappointingly few as compared with totals from the others of the 'Big Four'. Six A4s head the list though two are across the Atlantic, but after them the list is a short one since fate determined that LNER engines were sent to scrapyards which quickly broke them up. Only one (a B1) found its way to the South Wales graveyard from which so many other locomotives — especially of Southern and Great Western origin — were rescued. Nevertheless we can be grateful still to have representatives of Classes A3, A2, V2, K1, K4, B1 and D49 along with LNER versions of B12, N2 and N7, plus quite a good selection from the pre-grouping constituents. There are also some preserved teak-bodied carriages, a notable example being a restored Gresley buffet car in the National Collection; awaiting restoration are a 'Coronation' observation car and even, for our future delectation, a 'Quad-Art' set.

From the constituents, famous old company names can still be found — such as on the huge Great Northern Railway warehouse in Manchester or on the Cheshire Lines Committee goods shed at Warrington Central, all three partners being identified. Relics bearing physical testimony to the LNER are harder to spot but in fact there are plenty, if not at first recognised as such. The stations at West Monkseaton, Longbenton, Scunthorpe and Hertford North, to select a few examples, are LNER-built, as are the signal boxes at Barton Hill (between York and Scarborough), Harrogate, Hull Paragon and March South Junction, again among others, along with surviving LNER lattice post upper quadrant signals. Travelling on the ECML have you spotted the signs marking the halfway point, the 200 miles to London and Edinburgh, or the England/Scotland border? They were put there by the LNER.

Three Humber ferries are still around but special mention should be made of the paddle steamer *Waverley*, launched by the LNER in 1946 to replace a vessel of the same name sunk in 1940 during the Dunkirk evacuation. Still in working order in the care of a preservation trust, she continues to give pleasure cruising the Clyde coast and occasionally elsewhere around Britain.

Transition on the West Highland — K4 2-6-0 No.61995 Cameron of Lochiel crosses the River Lochy between Banavie and Mallaig Junction nearing Fort William with the 1.05pm from Mallaig to Glasgow Queen Street on 16th June 1951. Into the fourth year of nationalisation, the K4 clings to its LNER apple green livery and has kept the company's lettering on its tender despite being renumbered by BR and gaining a smokebox numberplate. The seven-coach train is similarly uncommitted, with four sporting the new BR crimson and cream and three remaining in LNER teak finish. (Eric Bruton)

The spirit of the LNER also survives in the running of today's railway system. The company which operates ECML expresses goes under the name Great North Eastern Railway (we will gloss over the fact that it doesn't actually *own* a railway!) and Network Rail, the infrastructure company, has a London North Eastern Zone as one of its operational areas. It is not hard to see from where they got their inspiration.

The three-cylinder D49 4-4-0s were conceived by the LNER as 'middle of the range' express engines for use in the North Eastern and Scottish Areas. However, in the post-war rush to return to apple green livery the D49s were overlooked completely and BR downgraded them by painting them in mixed traffic lined black. No. 62706 Forfarshire stands in front of the coaling plant at Darlington on 28th August 1948 before returning to Edinburgh Haymarket shed after a visit to the works. (J.W. Hague/D.V. Beeken collection)

LEFT:
NER J71 0-6-0T No. E8311 beetles energetically along the Leeds Northern main line at Monkton Moor on 27th March 1948. It has clearly just been repainted and the new State undertaking has lost no time in staking its claim to this pre-group shunting tank of 1895 vintage but the LNER number remains with the 'E' prefix. In fact, that was as far as No. 8311 got as it was scrapped in 1951 without it ever receiving its BR number. In the background can be glimpsed the flat-roofed signal box built during the war when the lay-by siding was converted into a loop to cope with the extra traffic of the time. (J.W. Hague/D.V. Beeken collection)

The D20 4-4-0s were introduced in 1899 by the North Eastern Railway — its distinguished Class R — and in their day represented that company's premier motive power on the East Coast route. Though cascaded down to secondary duties over the years, 50 of the 60 built passed into BR ownership and here we have No. 2384 on a local at Ripon in November 1948, not yet showing any indication of the new order. In fact, the engine has clearly come down in the world; whilst the latest LNER Gill Sans figures have been applied, it is still in wartime plain black and the brass beading to wheel splashers and cab windows remains unpolished. No. 2384 is allocated to Starbeck shed, Harrogate, which had ten D20s at the close the LNER era and the class was particularly familiar on the Leeds Northern line. Despite their express pedigree, BR did not feel the D20s warranted even mixed traffic lined black when it came to repainting them. Note the enamel signs which advertise Earle's Cement and Virol ("nursing mothers need it"), once common - place at stations large and small. (J.W. Hague/D.V. Beeken collection)

RIGHT:

B1 4-6-0 No. 61084 passes Thirsk with the 5.00pm Newcastle—Liverpool express composed of LMS stock repainted in an experimental livery of chocolate and cream. During the summer of 1948 fourteen trains were run by BR on a variety of routes in experimental colour schemes to gauge public opinion; the other livery trialled was a pseudo-LNWR style 'plum and spilt milk'. However, public opinion was not particularly gripped by the question and only around 1,000 people responded. In the end neither version was adopted and the first standard livery for main line stock was crimson and cream. B1 No. 61084 was one of an order from the North British Locomotive Co. which took to the rails in LNER lined black livery, though others of the class were turned out in green. More significantly, it was the first B1 to acquire BR lined black livery when repainted at Darlington in May 1948. (J.W. Hague/D.V. Beeken collection)

One of the most colourful episodes to occur in the first year of BR was the Locomotive Exchanges, staged by the Railway Executive ostensibly to try out various 'Big Four' designs on 'foreign' routes with a view to perpetuating the most 'successful'. Whether the trials actually achieved anything is debatable but they did certainly provide considerable excitement for enthusiasts in, for example, the sight of a Great Western 'King' 4-6-0 running between King's Cross and Leeds. No.6018 King Henry VI finds itself in the unfamiliar company of the NER dynamometer car and upper quadrant signals at Holbeck High Level, Leeds, on 18th May 1948. (J.W. Hague/D.V. Beeken collection)

2

TOP LINK

When it came to top-link passenger trains, the LNER in the pre-war years had been the glitziest of the 'Big Four'. The GWR had stately tradition and established respectability, the LMS had power, solidity and size, the Southern had its electric modernity, but the LNER had a dash of glamour that none of the others could quite match.

With its growing fleet of Mr. H.N. Gresley's Pacifics it followed its London—Newcastle non-stop service in 1927 by launching the non-stop London to Edinburgh run in 1928, the world's longest regular non-stop steam working. In 1934 No.4472 *Flying Scotsman,* already a celebrity on account of its display at the British Empire Exhibition and its role on the first Edinburgh non-stop, recorded the first undisputed British 100mph, a springboard to a heady spell of record-breaking. In 1935 the LNER trumped the others by presenting the country's first streamlined locomotives and trains: enter *Silver Link* and the unmistakeable shape of the A4 class and the 'Silver Jubilee' train to Newcastle, followed in 1937 by the 'Coronation' to Edinburgh and the 'West Riding' to Leeds and Bradford. 1938 saw *Mallard* rattle off its world speed record — 125 or 126mph as you prefer. It was an exhilarating time on the LNER (though it would not have thanked anyone for pointing out that whilst running stylish streamlined trains and observation cars it retained more six-wheel carriages during the 1930s than the rest put together!) but out in the wide world trouble was brewing and by the time 1939 closed we were engulfed in the Second World War.

Wartime saw main line passenger traffic relegated in importance as essential freight for the war effort was given priority. The streamlined trains were discontinued after 31st August, never to reappear; their coaches were put into storage to await the return of better times. The full story of the LNER's role during the dark days of 1939-45 is graphically told in the company's own book *By Rail to Victory.*

Come peace again in 1945 and the LNER was faced with the laborious task of bringing an exhausted railway back to pre-war standards. In 1946 it published a booklet entitled *Forward with the LNER* in which it set out the challenge ahead and (as the late Michael Harris wrote in *Backtrack* in 1993) specifically mentioned plans for the high speed trains, saying that "they will return just as soon as possible". But circumstances were such that they never did.

The Chief General Manager, Sir Charles Newton, seems to have been particularly keen on the high speed trains' return but the Passenger Managers' Committee was more cautious, for good practical reasons. Passenger numbers remained heavy even after the end of the war and so the streamlined trains, with their limited accommodation, were not really what the operators required at that time. Moreover, the condition of the track meant that the trains in any case would have had to run at a reduced speed until standards improved. Various options were considered but by the end of 1947 the LNER had already come to the conclusion that "present conditions were unpropitious" for the reintroduction of the high speed trains.

The incoming British Railways did find uses for the streamlined carriages but they never again ran together in their former glory. In 1948 the 'Silver Jubilee' restaurant car triplet set was put into a King's Cross—Newcastle working (as is illustrated on the front cover) and the other vehicles were sent north to work on the humble 'Fife Coast Express' between Glasgow and St. Andrews. 'Coronation' stock did reappear as part of East Coast route expresses and the "West Riding Limited' vehicles were put into a new 'West Riding' service.

One extremely positive development from the new BR was the resumption of the non-stop 'Flying Scotsman' between London and Edinburgh on 31st May 1948. The timings were inevitably slower than pre-war but disruption on a major scale came that August when massive flooding after several days' torrential rain over the Scottish borders breached the East Coast Main Line at a number of places, with no fewer than seven bridges washed away. Trains had to be diverted over alternative secondary routes in the Border country and, against the odds, several enterprising drivers still managed to craft non-stops runs despite the increased mileage. Military-type temporary bridges were erected as swiftly as possible and the ECML was able to be reopened on 1st November, though severe speed restrictions were applied over them until the following spring while new permanent bridges were being constructed. From the 1949 season the non-stop run was undertaken by a new train, the 'Capitals Limited' which was later renamed 'The Elizabethan' in 1953, Coronation year.

September 1948 saw the launch of the 'Tees-Tyne Pullman' between King's Cross, Darlington and Newcastle, as a partial substitution for the 'Silver Jubilee' of pre-war days. The same year a new service boosted the Great Central line — the

Three months into nationalisation but there is no evidence of it in this view of A3 Pacific No.46 **Diamond Jubilee** *approaching Potters Bar with an up semi-fast on Good Friday 26th March 1948. The locomotive is in full LNER apple green livery with its post-war number and the Gresley stock is in varnished teak. No.46 still has the right-hand driving position with which the first Gresley Pacifics were arranged; despite the increasing disadvantage of this in relation to the positioning of signals, it was left to British Railways to take the decision in 1951 to convert them to left-hand drive and No.46 was dealt with in October 1952. There are one or two signs of modernisation, though; the up fast line has been laid with flat-bottomed track which the LNER had first tried in 1939 and the distant signals are upper quadrant, these having been gradually adopted following recommendations made by the Institution of Railway Signal Engineers in 1924. The up fast distant is pushed out on the bracket for earlier sighting on the curve.* (Eric Bruton)

'South Yorkshireman' from Marylebone to Bradford via Sheffield and Huddersfield, joining the already popular 'Master Cutler' which the LNER had introduced between London and the steel city in 1947. As far as the latter was concerned, however, schedules between Marylebone and Sheffield remained considerably slower than those offered before the war, though the reputation of the 'Master Cutler' benefited from its being faster than the best train on the Midland route. The 'Queen of Scots' Pullman (King's Cross to Glasgow via Leeds and Edinburgh) was also reinstated in 1948. In 1949 the previously-mentioned 'West Riding' began as did the 'White Rose' and various named services in Scotland — the 'Bon Accord', 'Granite City' and 'Fife Coast Express' — were launched, all adding to the suggestion that the railway was picking itself up and recovering.

Not, though, during the period reviewed in this book did speeds start getting back to pre-war levels. The new 'White Rose' service, for instance, left London at 9.18am and, despite running non-stop to Doncaster, did not reach Leeds until 1.11pm, seven minutes under four hours — 233 minutes for 185¾ miles. The southbound run was even worse; after departing from Leeds at 5.15pm it took a miserable 4½ hours to reach King's Cross and when the Leeds departure was brought forward to 3.15pm the journey time was actually increased by eleven minutes. The continuing poor condition of the permanent way as a consequence of the arrears of maintenance during the war was largely to blame for the lethargic schedules but the unreliability of the top link locomotive fleet was also a significant factor. A one-off trial high speed return run was made by an A4 in May 1949, a sign

A year on from the previous picture and the scene is still as LNER as ever as A4 4-6-2 No.26 Miles Beevor hurries the 10.00am express from Newcastle to King's Cross through the cutting between Brookman's Park and Potters Bar on 9th April 1949. The photographer notes the time as 3.12pm, so any post-war acceleration has not exactly affected this train! The A4 is in garter blue LNER livery with new number applied in stainless steel figures, pre-war style, and lacks only the valancing over the wheels which had been removed during the war; it was renamed from Kestrel in November 1947 as a result of a board decision to indulge its senior officers and directors by naming locomotives after them. The train, too, remains in LNER livery; the first three vehicles are Thompson-designed carriages in ersatz teak finish followed by a triplet restaurant car set in real teak, and LNER-style white roofboards are carried. (Eric Bruton)

---

that the authorities were aware of the need to improve the dilatory timetables, but the civil engineers were not yet ready to countenance faster running on a regular basis; not until 1951 was 90mph permitted on any stretch of the ECML, though by 1953 schedules were noticeably improving. The extent of the service offered was decidedly thin as well, with no train from London to Newcastle and Edinburgh before 9.30am in the first British Railways timetable. Incredible as it seems today, the last daytime departure to Edinburgh was at 1.00pm with nothing for Newcastle between then and 3.30. It was fortunate for the railways, if not for passengers, that they still enjoyed a virtual monopoly on long-distance travel and so

The LNER embarked on the restoration of apple green livery to its A1/A3 Pacifics in 1946 and managed to get most of them done before nationalisation; the handful remaining were turned out by British Railways. This view of **Tracery** *on the turntable at King's Cross loco yard on 21st February 1949 shows it has gained its BR number and ownership markings. Note also the route availability rating 'RA9' which applied to lines over which the heaviest locomotives were permitted to run; this system had been generally adopted throughout the LNER in 1947 and it was subsequently perpetuated by BR.* (BR/Pendragon collection)

could get away with the dismal service provided; serious competition, though, lay round the corner.

How stood the East Coast motive power fleet during the LNER/BR transitional years? Dominating the scene, of course, were Sir Nigel Gresley's Pacifics — 78 of the A1/A3 class and 34 of the streamlined A4s. Both classes had been depleted by one — an A4 had been destroyed in the York air raid of 1942 and an A1 had been rebuilt by Edward Thompson as the basis for a new standard Pacific. All were concentrated at the principal East Coast route depots apart from nine A3s allocated to the GC route in 1949. Supporting them were the 184 members of the splendidly-versatile V2 2-6-2 class.

Thompson had succeeded Gresley following the latter's death in 1941 and LNER enthusiasts have tended not to regard

A4 No.60021 **Wild Swan** *bursts forth from Hadley Wood South Tunnel with the 10.00am from Newcastle on 23rd April 1949, with just a wisp of steam showing as it descends the 1 in 200 gradient. Garter blue livery remains but the A4 has gained its new owners' insignia and a smokebox numberplate; being a Gateshead-based engine, it lacks the higher standards of polish which were reappearing from some other depots at that time. This time the photographer notes the time as 4.07pm; as post-war schedules struggled to recover, passengers are six hours into the journey from Newcastle and still not in London! Note the Milepost 14 angled back to suit the driver's angle of view, the wooden frame on the right to carry a cable run over the tunnel and the telegraph lines also taking a route above the tunnel.* (Eric Bruton)

A3 No.60055 **Woolwinder** *charges towards Welwyn Garden City with the Sunday 11.20am King's Cross—Glasgow express in a fine action shot taken on 5th March 1950. The locomotive still carries the apple green of its old company and the leading steel-bodied vehicle clearly shows the painted teak effect finish which the LNER applied to Thompson stock. It now has an 'E' prefix added to the number in the same style.* (Eric Bruton)

his tenure of office as a happy one — unjustly to some extent. In 1943 his first Pacifics (Class A2/2) had been created by rebuilding Gresley's P2 2-8-2 (designed for use on the East Coast route north of Edinburgh) as 4-6-2s with three separate sets of valve gear preferred by Thompson as opposed to the expensive-to-maintain derived motion which had been favoured by his predecessor. The following year four V2s on order were cancelled and their boilers and frames used for another Pacific design (A2/1). Neither of these types can be said to have covered itself in any particular glory, but Thompson's eventual standard mixed traffic Pacific (A2/3) turned out to be quite good. His controversial rebuilding of the pioneer A1 *Great Northern* (mentioned earlier) led to a new standard A1 Pacific which was developed and constructed under his successor Arthur Peppercorn who has received the credit for an excellent design.

Thompson was in favour of standardising the LNER's fleet of locomotives and a 'Five Year Plan' from 1945 envisaged future construction revolving around ten standard classes, with a further nine classes being reboilered and maintained. His best-known and probably most useful legacy was, however, the mixed traffic B1 4-6-0 which proved in every way a match for the outstandingly successful GWR 'Halls' and LMS Class 5s of comparable power classification. The first allocation of B1s to the GN line was to Hitchin in the autumn on 1946 for use on outer suburban trains, though they were often appropriated for main line expresses to relieve failed Pacifics at a time when the latter's performance was causing problems. They soon acquired some quite important assignments such as the Cambridge buffet expresses and the Cleethorpes—King's Cross return service.

continued on page 22

A new Pacific class featured in Edward Thompson's standardisation plans for the LNER but it was not until after he had retired and been succeeded by Arthur Peppercorn that the design was finalised and it was under BR auspices that the A1 Class entered service on the East Coast Main Line. This photograph of No.60130, taken at King's Cross shed on 15th February 1949 when it was just five months old, shows what a handsome machine it was. The minimalist chimney which the A1s received at first, with just a beading around the rim, perhaps detracted from their appearance but full-lip chimneys were fitted later. Most of them were given apple green livery though they wore it but briefly before being repainted in the new BR blue; the LNER green seems to have suited them nevertheless. At first the A1s were anonymous but between 1950 and 1951 nameplates were fitted and No.60130 became *Kestrel*, taking a name discarded from an A4. In the background is a V2 2-6-2 No.60821 still in wartime black. (BR/Pendragon collection)

A1 No.60136 departs from King's Cross and prepares to plunge into the murk of Gasworks Tunnel with the 11.30am 'Queen of Scots' Pullman to Glasgow on 2nd July 1949. With eight months' work behind it, No.60136 (named **Alcazar** the following year) has gathered a coating of dust and grime, a sign that pre-war standards of cleanliness were not always achievable in the transitional years. The brass handrail and door handle of the Pullman car have been polished, however! (Eric Bruton)

A4 No.60023 **Golden Eagle** *leads the up midday Newcastle—King's Cross express past Marshmoor on 18th April 1948. The locomotive is still in the 'intermediate LNER-BR' turnout but this time has its new number painted LNER-style across the bottom of the streamlined front casing, while all the train — including the Thompson steel-panelled brake composite behind the tender— is in teak finish. In the foreground is a rotating ground signal to give access from the down slow line into the goods yard and private sidings, while beyond that is a relay cubicle.* (Eric Bruton)

A shaft of sunlight penetrates the habitual gloom and smoke at Liverpool Street at 2.55pm on the afternoon of 25th August 1948. An express for Cromer has been brought into Platform 9 by a B12 4-6-0 and a vintage LNER refreshment trolley awaits customers. At the back of the station is the famous Great Eastern Hotel in front of which extends a footbridge to the hotel entrance and the eastern section of the station. Suspended from the roof are information signs in the clear Gill Sans alphabet devised specifically for the LNER; the 'Post and Telegram Office' takes us back to how we used to communicate from stations long before the mobile phone era! A passenger squints up at the departure board which was mounted on a footbridge at this point along the platform. (Eric Bruton)

The 7.50am express from Leeds and Bradford swings round the reverse curve from Hatfield towards Red Hall box on 16th April 1949, with A1 No.60134 comfortably in charge. The train is wholly LNER including the immaculate leading Gresley carriage, with external doors to each compartment and newly-painted white roof; how long it would remain like that is a matter of conjecture! LNER white roofboards are carried further down the train. No.60134 was one of the Darlington-built A1s five months into its career; in October 1950 it acquired the name Foxhunter, *one of the A1s to perpetuate the old LNER tradition of commemorating racehorses.* (Eric Bruton)

In 1946 Thompson retired, to be succeeded by Peppercorn. The new A1 Pacifics, though attributed to him, were largely the work of Thompson and had first been authorised in the 1945 construction programme. It was left to Peppercorn to modify the design details, not least in tidying up the outward appearance of the class, such that the A1 Class became an extremely handsome machine in the true LNER tradition — and much more to enthusiasts' taste! But though it was a wholly LNER concept, it was left to BR to put the new A1 Pacifics into traffic since the first did not make its debut until August 1948 and construction continued until the end of 1949.

At this time the prestigious fleet of A4 and A3 Pacifics was in a rundown condition as a result of wartime overwork and neglect and the situation was exacerbated by the shortage of maintenance staff, particularly at King's Cross. The new A1s, strong and reliable, played a valuable role in keeping the ECML running during a difficult period.

A smoky haze emerges from under the roof at King's Cross but almost new A2 4-6-2 No. 60533 Happy Knight has found the sun as it starts away with the 3.50pm 'Yorkshire Pullman' for Leeds and Harrogate on 25th August 1948, observed by an engineman in grease-top cap and bicycle clips on his overalls. The use of the Peppercorn A2s on top link work to and from King's Cross was not particularly common and was fairly short-lived as they mostly tended to inhabit the northern end of the ECML and Scotland, but No. 60533 was one of three new A2s to spend six months or so working from Copley Hill shed, Leeds, on London expresses in 1948. Its livery is apple green and it is one of only two to carry its BR number on the front bufferbeam. Note the luggage barrows lined up on the right, behind which is a trolley piled high with parcels awaiting the next empty stock into the platform. On the far platform more trolleys await loading from a newly-arrived train from Newcastle which has brought in a couple of sailors amongst its passengers. (Eric Bruton)

A delightful shot encompassing old and new at Hadley South Tunnel where apple green A1 No.60134 heading the up 'Yorkshire Pullman' is beckoned onwards to Greenwood by GNR somersault signals on 23rd April 1949. Most of the A1s were fitted with electric lighting equipment, worked by a turbo-generator on the running plate partly hidden by the right-hand smoke deflector. However, it remained obligatory for traditional oil lamps to be carried during daylight so that signalmen could identify the train classification. The Pullmans are the steel cars built for this service in 1928; the second and fifth vehicles are kitchen cars for serving the adjoining carriages. A detail worth mentioning is a new cable run on concrete posts on the cutting side, possibly to replace the older one on wooden posts close to the track. Note might also be made of the well-trimmed banks of the steam age, very different to the overgrown tracksides of today! The single signal arm on the bracket controls access to the up slow line at Greenwood where four-track running resumes; later in the 1950s BR set about getting rid of this two-track bottleneck by widening the section between Potters Bar and Greenwood, a project which included additional tunnels at Potters Bar, Hadley Wood North and Hadley Wood South. (Eric Bruton)

In 1951 the Eastern Region decided to improve the situation by basing all its A4s at King's Cross and allocating regular crews to them. This was a reintroduction of an old practice going back to Great Northern days and once commonplace on many railways. The theory was that regular manning would help to ensure that the A4s were kept in the best possible condition with crews taking special pride in 'their' engines. As Peter Townend, shedmaster at King's Cross, wrote in *Top Shed:* "The regular manning of A4s worked very well and helped everyone get the best out of the locomotives at a time when many of the Pacifics were giving performances below their pre-war best".

On the Great Eastern main line the principal motive power had, since 1928, been the B17 'Sandringham' class 4-6-0s. Designing a powerful three-cylinder 4-6-0 which complied with the GE Section's axle load limitations proved a tricky proposition and the North British Locomotive Co. of Glasgow was entrusted with drawing up the design. Following

Thompson's appointment he prepared plans for the rebuilding of the B17s as two-cylinder engines with his new standard boiler. It is not surprising that he did not see a complicated three-cylinder 4-6-0 figuring in his standardisation plans but he did foresee the perpetuation of his rebuilt version (Class B2) in view of its particular suitability for GE line expresses and to a lesser extent elsewhere. The rebuilding programme began in 1945 and eight more engines had been dealt with by the close of the LNER era. BR converted one more in 1949 but the success of the B1 mixed traffic 4-6-0s led the motive power authorities to conclude that these versatile new locomotives were better suited to modern needs and the rebuilding of the B17s was abandoned.

So in the immediate transitional years the main GE express trains remained in the capable yet traditional care of the 'Sandringhams', but change lay around the corner. In 1949 the abundance (some would say over-abundance) of Southern Railway light Pacifics prompted the Railway Executive to

OPPOSITE PAGE

A4 No.60015 **Quicksilver** *takes a course out of York heading north on 16th July 1950 with a very mixed train of empty stock authorised to run under Class A headcode. The leading vehicle is of particular interest, being one of the substantially-constructed Great Central Railway 'Barnum' carriages dating from 1910. No.60015 — one of the four original silver A4s — has acquired the first BR livery for principal express locomotives, blue with black and white lining. It is allocated to Grantham, a reminder that this was once an important railway centre with a busy depot which had a number of top link duties; around this time Grantham shed and men worked the down 'Flying Scotsman' from there to Newcastle. The York station area is in the throes of the resignalling which was commissioned the following year; two new steel gantries for colour lights have been erected and in the foreground a new ground signal has been installed to replace the North Eastern Railway shunting signal. Note also the two enginemen walking along the track towards the station, demonstrating why high-visibility clothing was eventually to be such a good idea.* (Eric Bruton)

The 'Flying Scotsman' reverted to non-stop running between London and Edinburgh in 1948 for one summer only; from 1949 the non-stop was undertaken by a new train, the 'Capitals Limited', and the 'Scotsman' made calls at Grantham and Newcastle. This photograph of No.60010 **Dominion of Canada** *working hard on the up train passing Yaxley is undated but must be after September 1950 when No.60010 gained BR blue livery; it is, however, still carrying the old LNER headboard, a bit battered-looking by now. The locomotive's bell had been presented by the Canadian Pacific Railway in 1938 and was originally steam-operated. However, just before the war it was made unusable after a driver had been unable to stop it after ringing it on leaving King's Cross in response to a request from an enthusiast; the bell continued ringing all the way to York! It remained in place, though, until removed in 1957 when a double chimney was fitted. The gradual repainting of carriages in BR crimson and cream livery has robbed trains of a unified appearance during the transition between full LNER and BR colour schemes.* (Pendragon collection)

wonder if these under-used engines might be more gainfully employed on the GE main lines, to which end one was sent for a month's loan in order to see how it shaped up. The trial was presumably inconclusive and nothing further happened until May 1951 when three were allocated to Stratford. Their use on the GE was, however, a side issue for the new British Railways had been busy drawing up schemes for a range of new standard locomotives, the first manifestation being a Class 7 4-6-2 which made its appearance in 1951. The pioneer member of the class was given the name *Britannia* and the locomotives were soon widely known as the 'Britannia' Pacifics.

The first of the class was allocated to the Eastern Region for use on trains between Liverpool Street, Ipswich and Norwich, on which they were the first Pacifics to see regular service. More importantly, they were the most powerful locomotives yet seen on the GE lines and their arrival was eagerly anticipated. A regular interval service began between London and Norwich on 2nd July 1951 with generally accelerated timings. The operating authorities and footplatemen seized the opportunity the new motive power offered them and the best trains became faster than the best on the Western Region main line to Bristol; for a while the down 'Broadsman' was the fastest train in the United Kingdom.

The 'Broadsman' was a new named train inaugurated in 1950, running between Liverpool Street, Norwich and Cromer. It joined the 'East Anglian' — an LNER title restored in 1946 — and the 'Norfolkman' — introduced in 1948 — in the London to Norwich timetable. The 'Hook Continental' was another long-established train, reinstated after the war, linking Liverpool Street with Harwich Parkeston Quay and the steamer to the Hook of Holland.

continued on page 30

Another chance to soak up the sulphurous atmosphere of Liverpool Street in the post-war steam years. This is another view on 25th August 1948 of the Cromer train seen in the earlier picture but this time from the buffer-end of Platform 9 looking towards the 'tumbleover' arrival and departure indicator mounted on the long footbridge which spanned both western and eastern sections of the station. Passengers and railway staff flit between light and shade as the empty stock engine, whose identity the photographer did not record, festers away at the rear of the train attracting the attention of a young enthusiast who is in conversation with the driver. (Eric Bruton)

As mentioned, 'The Capitals Limited' took over from 'The Flying Scotsman' as the London—Edinburgh non-stop train from the 1949 season and ran ahead as a relief to it departing at 9.30am. Top Shed's No.60025 *Falcon* erupts from Hadley Wood North Tunnel with the northbound train on 8th September 1951 on the 1 in 200 gradient to Potters Bar summit. The A4 is in BR blue livery and the leading Thompson brake in red and cream, a rather jarring combination perhaps. The second vehicle is still in pseudo-teak finish. The 'Capitals' was a short-lived name as in 1953 the train was retitled 'The Elizabethan' in honour of Coronation year, a name which survived until the service ended in 1962. At the time of this photograph, however, the ailing King George VI was still on the throne and the new Elizabethan age was still five months away. (Eric Bruton)

The LNER launched the 'Master Cutler' service from Marylebone to Sheffield in 1947 but it was BR which gave the Great Central line an allocation of A3 Pacifics in 1949 after an absence of some years. No.60052 **Prince Palatine** *pulls out of Marylebone at 6.15pm with the down train, composed of Gresley stock in the new livery, on 21st July 1949. However, it would be turned ten o'clock before Sheffield was reached.* (Locomotive Club of Great Britain/Ken Nunn collection 7736)

ABOVE

Edinburgh should not be regarded as the end of the East Coast route as the North British main lines continued north to Dundee and Aberdeen as well as west to Glasgow. Having arrived at Glasgow Queen Street with the 1.00pm express from Edinburgh on 9th June 1951, A2 No.60529 Pearl Diver *provides formidable banking power as the unseen station pilot takes the empty stock up the gradient of Cowlairs bank. No.60529 is a Haymarket engine fitted with multiple valve regulator, the linkage of which runs along the top of the boiler. The A2s were not designated as one of the principal express classes accorded blue livery by BR and went straight into Brunswick green. Spanning the station is a beautifully symmetrical signal gantry with each post having an exit and approach arm for each platform.* (Eric Bruton)

When in Edinburgh a favourite spot for train watching and photography was in Prince's Street Gardens where a couple of lattice footbridges spanned the lines west of Waverley station between The Mound and Haymarket Tunnels. Just after ten o'clock on 8th June 1951 the photographer was well placed to record two simultaneous 10.00am departures from Waverley: blue A4 No.60011 **Empire of India** *on the Aberdeen train accelerates vigorously away from A3 No.60054* **Prince of Wales** *which is bound for Glasgow Queen Street. Gresley vehicles make up most of the Aberdeen train and garish paint has largely covered the hitherto varnished woodwork.* (Eric Bruton)

Early in 1949 BR wondered if more productive use could be made of the Southern Region Light Pacifics by putting some of them to work on the Great Eastern line and to see how they might shape up, 'Battle of Britain' No.34059 **Sir Archibald Sinclair** *was sent on loan to Stratford shed at the end of April to undertake some trial running. On 18th May (still in post-war Southern Railway malachite green livery) it was entrusted with the prestigious 'Norfolkman' service between Liverpool Street and Norwich on which it was photographed making volcanic progress on the climb towards Ingrave summit with the down train. The allocation of no fewer than fifteen SR Pacifics was suggested but by the end of May No.34059 was back home and there was no immediate outcome to the trials. As mentioned in the text, five Light Pacifics later spent several months on the GE in 1951 but whilst the appearance of such exotic motive power doubtless delighted enthusiasts, the opinions of enginemen were decidedly mixed. The power of the engines, their free-steaming boilers and smooth riding characteristics were appreciated but the usual hostility towards 'foreign' engines militated against them and they were certainly reckoned to be high on coal consumption.* (F.G. Hebron/ Rail Archive Stephenson)

OPPOSITE PAGE BOTTOM:
B2 4-6-0 No.61632 **Belvoir Castle** *— one of Thompson's two-cylinder rebuilds of the 'Sandringham' three-cylinder class — attacks Brentwood bank with the 10.30am Liverpool Street—Clacton buffet car express on 24th March 1951. It is expending much effort on the 1 in 65 gradient to Ingrave summit but the photographer logged it as passing at about 20mph, so it may have been slowed or even stopped at Brentwood. Above the tracks are the wires of the Shenfield 1,500V dc electrification which had been completed two years before. In 1950 the Clacton service was put on a regular interval basis departing from Liverpool Street at 30 minutes past the hour, with the working being shared by B2s based at Colchester and B1s from Stratford. The capability of the latter put an end to the conversion of further B17s into B2s after 1949.* (Eric Bruton)

This scene is British Railways through and through. In 1951 its new 'Britannia' 4-6-2s burst upon the Great Eastern main line and No. 70002 Geoffrey Chaucer hustles the up 'Norfolkman' from Norwich past Shenfield en route to Liverpool Street. The modern traction is complemented by the up-to-date rolling stock, for the train is composed entirely of new BR Mark I coaches in the crimson and cream colour scheme. The 'Norfolkman' was one of the 'Festival of Britain Trains' which BR announced as using only these latest carriages. Note the continuing use of headcode discs rather than lamps on the GE line and the handrails on the smoke deflectors of the 'Britannia', later removed in favour of cut-out grab holds after an accident on the Western Region when it was claimed that the handrails obstructed the driver's forward view. (NRM/P. Ransome-Wallis X826)

Hardly had the 'Britannias' made their debut on the GE, however, than they had to be withdrawn due to problems arising in the middle of 1951 from coupled wheels shifting on their axles. All were taken out of service on 27th October 1951 for modification, returning to traffic between 1st December and the following February. During these few months the operators struggled to maintain the 'Britannia' schedules with B1 and B17 4-6-0s, along with a couple of the new BR Standard Class 5s; although it was not possible to uphold the timetables, there was nevertheless some spirited effort. Five Southern Railway 'Battle of Britain' Pacifics (the three allocated to Stratford and two sent on loan to help with the emergency) also pitched in, mostly on the Harwich and Cambridge runs, but there was great relief when the 'Britannias' were all back at work. The SR Pacifics were sent home, largely unmissed. Since the 'Britannia' Pacifics never made any significant inroads on the ECML, over which LNER Pacifics ruled until steam's demise, it was on Great Eastern line expresses where the transition from LNER to BR practice was first completed.

What rolling stock was on the trains during these years of transition? The LNER bequeathed the teak-bodied stock of the Gresley era and some newer steel-panelled vehicles introduced by Thompson which had a curious teak-effect paint finish to match them to the polished teak of the earlier carriages. Whilst no doubt expensive to achieve, this pseudo-teak finish was perhaps understandable in avoiding the clash of mixed liveries which was to disrupt the harmonious

appearance of trains during the various transitional periods through which the railways have passed (not just post-nationalisation but also in the late 1960s and again in the 1980s/'90s); yet the opportunity to devise an exciting new, modern livery was missed. Early in 1949 British Railways announced a new colour scheme of crimson and cream for main line coaching stock and the LNER vehicles soon began to appear in this as they passed through the works; doubtless burying the cherished polished teak beneath a brash new paint scheme came hard to some paintshop craftsmen.

The B1 mixed traffic 4-6-0s performed some outstanding work on the Great Central route and even after the A3 Pacifics made a reappearance in 1949 they had many top link workings, including most of those over the difficult section between Sheffield and Manchester via Woodhead before its electrification. No.61162 has called at Penistone with the 10.00am Manchester London Road—Marylebone on 7th April 1950. In the background can be seen the platform of the former Lancashire & Yorkshire Railway branch to Huddersfield, today the only line serving Penistone following the abandonment of the Woodhead route. (T.J. Edgington)

OPPOSITE PAGE LOWER

There is a wintry feel to the railway on 27th January 1951, with frost on sleepers and rails, as A1 No.60128 Bongrace *whisks the 8.24am Grantham—King's Cross past the down line signals near Red Hall box, south of Hatfield. This was one of the last batch of Doncaster-built A1s completed between May and December 1949 which never got to wear LNER apple green but went straight into BR blue livery; it had acquired its name (another racehorse!) the previous November. Lineside interest is provided by the lattice signal bracket with splitting distant signals and the wooden permanent way gangers' hut.* (Eric Bruton)

An extraordinary interlude at this time was the adventure in 1949 of some novel vehicles described as tavern cars. These had half their exteriors in the standard new crimson and cream but the other half was finished in an extraordinary ersatz brickwork effect on the lower panel and pseudo stucco and half-timbering above, with a pub sign bearing names such as 'At the sign of the White Horse'. Within was a bar in a sort of timbered mock-Tudor style where, amongst other delights, beer could be served from the barrel.

On the Eastern Region tavern cars with accompanying restaurant car were precipitated on to the 'Master Cutler' between Marylebone and Sheffield, the 'White Rose' between King's Cross and Leeds, the 'Norfolkman', the 'South Yorkshireman' and the Harwich—Liverpool boat train. The vehicles were of Southern Railway origin to the design of its chief mechanical engineer O.V.S. Bulleid; their use had been expected to be confined to the Southern Region and the Railway Executive's decision, in its wisdom, to spread their allocation more widely seems to have somewhat surprised the Eastern. The tavern cars sparked considerable controversy, centred on complaints of discomfort, bad design and poor taste, and in 1950 they were all transferred to the SR for which they had originally been intended.

In the same year as the first of the Standard range of locomotives made its debut, there also appeared the first of British Railways' new standard carriages, designated Mark I. They were, in many ways, not particularly imaginative vehicles but they were robust and durable in the manner of much post-war design and continued to be constructed, in a wide range of

A dramatic shot of blue-liveried A4 No. 60033 Seagull *sweep-ing under the bridge at the northern end of Langley troughs, south of Stevenage, and starting to scoop up water at 60mph at the head of an up express on 3rd November 1951. No. 60033 is a Top Shed engine, one of the final three A4s built which had double blastpipe and chimneys from new. Langley troughs (provided only on the fast lines) were the first of the six sets on the ECML going north at only some 27 miles out of London but having troughs so close to King's Cross enabled locomotives on short turn-rounds to avoid the need to take water at the terminus. Look at the height of that telegraph post!* (Eric Bruton)

formats, for more than a decade. BR decreed that some new titled trains for Festival of Britain year in 1951 would be wholly composed of the new stock and on the ECML the 2.00pm King's Cross—Edinburgh (and vice versa) gained the name "Heart of Midlothian". The new MkI coaches were also

put into the 'Norfolkman' on the GE main line. BR stock soon began to displace LNER vehicles on the principal trains; whilst they had comfortable well-sprung seats and a layout which matched them with wide windows — concepts now apparently lost of designers! — they were very traditional in ambience and lacking in the contemporary style which had characterised the best of the LNER's new stock of pre-war days.

So during the years from 1948 to 1952 the transition was marked by only gradual change; new motive power was mostly LNER in origin and the top link types which had reigned before the war continued to do so afterwards, while the new Standard locomotives would not make their presence felt on the ECML for some time yet. Old liveries slowly yielded to new ones and only towards the end of our period did BR's new rolling stock start to oust that taken over from the LNER. Many might well have thought it was still the LNER with a different name...

A4 No.60008 **Dwight D. Eisenhower** *blasts north near Welwyn Garden City with an unidentified down express, probably a Christmas extra, on 24th December 1953. This photograph dates from a year later than our nominal transitional period but not only is it a fine picture with which to end this section but it also enables us to show LNER top link motive power in its final BR condition, painted in the green livery which displaced blue from 1951. Thereafter the only change would be the use of the later tender crest after about 1957. This 'going away' shot reveals that No.60008 is paired with a corridor tender as evidenced by the port - hole window and the roof of the corridor running along the right-hand side of the tender. The steam drifting up from the front of the tender shows that the fireman is using the slacker pipe to wet the coal with hot water and so keep down the dust. Through the cab window can be glimpsed the back of the fireman's leather-padded 'bucket'-type seat, Gresley having been one of the very few locomotive engineers to give much consideration to the comfort of footplatemen.* (Eric Bruton)

3

WHEELS OF INDUSTRY

Mention of the LNER nearly always tends to conjure up images of Gresley's Pacific locomotives, streamlined trains, speed records, famous names. But in truth all these were in the way of sideshows as far as the railway's real business was concerned; the LNER was essentially a freight railway and earned some two-thirds of its income from goods traffic.

Coal was at the forefront of this. Many of the pits in the huge south Yorkshire coalfield were served by the former Great Northern lines in the area, while the once mighty Durham and Northumberland coalfield also generated a substantial volume of traffic as did the mines of the east Midlands and Fifeshire. Huge tonnages of coal were required by industry especially for power generation and it must also be remembered that most homes were heated by coal fires. Remarkable also in the light of changes over the last couple of decades was the tonnage of coal exported, in particular from Immingham — today *imported* coal is *landed* there! — although export coal had been declining in volume during LNER days.

The engineering industries required the transport of iron ore, limestone and coal, then sent out its products. Fish traffic was of great importance as the LNER and its successor BR Regions served the great East Coast fishing ports of Aberdeen, Hull and Grimsby amongst many others. The LNER had been speeding up its main express goods trains before the war, with a growing number of fully-braked wagons, and fish trains sped their way south overnight to ensure morning deliveries at the markets.

The speedier express goods trains also brought benefits to the important agricultural industry which dominated the eastern counties and the Scottish meat industry. The operation of express fitted freights for 'perishables' was given high priority and trains such as the famous 'Scotch Goods', leaving King's Cross goods depot in the late afternoon, were briskly timed to ensure the arrival of perishables in Glasgow for the next morning's markets.

By the 1930s, however, the LNER had come to face increasing competition from the road haulage industry. While for bulk haulage over longer distances the railway maintained its advantages, for shorter distances lorries were proving to be more and more attractive on account of their flexibility and economy. Although the 1933 Road & Rail Traffic Act had brought in commercial vehicle licensing, road operators were able to set their own charges. Railways, on the other hand, were bound by legal obligations to (amongst other things) publish their charges, act as common carriers (ie accept any goods offered), afford 'reasonable facilities' and show no undue preference. Unhampered by the railways' need to base tariffs on the value of the goods to be carried, road hauliers could charge according to the actual cost of their service. The 1933 Act did at least relieve railways of the need to charge all customers equally and not to show undue preference by allowing them to negotiate 'agreed charges' with individual traders, but all such arrangements still had to be approved by the Railway Rates Tribunal. Just before the war the LNER had been actively engaged in the 'Square Deal Campaign' in which the 'Big Four' companies sought to obtain from the Government the freedom to scrap charging restrictions and compete openly with road hauliers on what we would now call a 'level playing field'.

This competition was one of the commercial motivations for the LNER's acceleration of long-distance express freights, alongside the practical one of cutting congestion of busy main lines, but on many secondary routes and branch lines goods trains, largely unbraked, pursued a slow and ponderous course. In terms of freight haulage, little really changed in the transitional period. The fortunes of various industries waxed and waned, their railway business likewise, but there were to be few changes in operational practice.

Before long, however, the growth of the road haulage industry — not least as more and more firms set up their own distribution fleets — and the improvement of the road network would challenge British Railways for practically every form of freight traffic on offer. The 1947 Transport Act also brought about nationalisation of the road haulage industry and dangled the notion of 'integrated public transport' before the public good — not for the last time! The British Transport Commission began acquiring haulage companies in 1948 and its annual report for 1951 showed that its British Road Services fleet then totalled 44,000 vehicles. BRS set out to capture long-distance traffic and formed, for the first time, a national trunk network of road service and depots which industry found of considerable benefit when considering transport options. However, the 'C' licence vehicles — those used by businesses for their own carriage — were not covered by the nationalisation and continued to

proliferate unrestrained, while many other vehicles, such as tankers and those used for furniture, meat and livestock, were also excluded, all of which undermined the whole concept of integration. Furthermore, the general election of 1951 saw the return of a Conservative government with a quite different political attitude towards public transport and any tenuous prospects of real integration disappeared in 1953 with the denationalisation of road haulage.

Not surprisingly, British Railways was handed a substantial stock of freight motive power by the LNER in 1948, much of it coming down from pre-grouping days. Steam locomotives are by nature long-lasting and many of the robust goods designs continued to meet the needs for heavy grind, local pick-up work or shunting without any incentive for their replacement. The North Eastern Railway, a predominantly mineral railway, had developed a range of 0-6-0 and 0-8-0 classes which on most duties remained unchallenged; two of its designs — to be designated J27 and Q6 in the LNER classification — could be seen at work until the end of steam in the north east in 1967. The same applied to the North British Railway's admirable 0-6-0s, which finally disappeared only a year earlier.

The Great Northern and Great Central, both with long hauls over their main lines, moved to 2-8-0s and the latter company

The three-cylinder K3 Class 2-6-0 express goods locomotives originated on the Great Northern Railway in 1920 but most were built by the LNER between 1924 and 1937. No.61862 has emerged from Hadley Wood South Tunnel on 23rd April 1949 and is about to take the up slow line at Greenwood signal box as directed by the splitting signal arm. The train is a block load of bricks from Fletton running under Class J headcode for a mineral train. The leading wagon is an LNER 50-ton bogie brick wagon built for that specific trade. 25 fully-fitted 50-ton brick wagons had been introduced by the GNR in 1921 for traffic from the London Brick Co. at Fletton, near Peterborough, and were branded 'Load 50 tons Distributed'. The LNER just branded their later versions 'Brick' or 'Brick - Return to Fletton'. All were painted red oxide. Note how the signal arms on the main post have become tilted upwards as a result of wear in the arm stop. (Eric Bruton)

produced one of the most successful goods engines ever in the shape of its Class 8K, LNER/BR Class O4. First appearing in 1911, it was taken up in the First World War by the Railway Operating Division of the Royal Engineers which ordered 521 of them for use at home and in France and Belgium. No fewer than 273 of these were subsequently purchased by the LNER.

continued on page 41

The use of Pacific locomotives on express goods work was commonplace and here we have A1 No.60117, still in LNER green and unnamed, south of Welwyn Garden City on 5th March 1950 with the late Saturday night/Sunday morning 11.45pm Edinburgh to King's Cross Goods vans. Between the tracks and on the outside of the slow line are dwarf banner repeater signals seen from the rear, a type of signal not now seen. (Eric Bruton)

Another round of coal goes into the firebox of K3 No.61954 as it pounds along the up slow line at Langley, near Stevenage, on 12th May 1951 with a Class K mixed goods which shunts at intermediate stations. The first two wagons carry containers, a form of freight handling which the LNER had been promoting from the late 1920s. The K3, from New England shed at Peterborough, is in deplorable external condition, a measure of how in the post-war years the railway found it difficult to find staff to clean engines, other than top link passenger motive power, to the standards previously known. The van standing in the siding on the right of the picture is a weighing machine van used by Messrs. Pooley Ltd. for adjusting weighbridges and other weighing equipment at stations and goods depots. On the main line the 70mph speed limit sign shows that speeds are improving into the 1950s; a lower speed limit will have applied through Stevenage station and over Langley troughs. (Eric Bruton)

OPPOSITE PAGE:
The Cheshire Lines Committee route between Liverpool and Manchester has never attracted photographers to any great extent but it was an important link between the two cities, providing the fastest passenger service and carrying some of the large volume of freight which passed between them and points east. This is Padgate station, east of Warrington, on 17th October 1953 with ex-Great Central D11/1 'Improved Director' 4-4-0 No.62663 Prince Albert trundling through from the Liverpool direction on a menial Class H goods. Once the pride of GC route expresses, No.62663 has certainly come down in the world, nor has it seen a cleaner's rag for some time. First introduced in 1919, the D11 class was perpetuated by the LNER in 1924 with the building of another two dozen for use on the North British lines in Scotland where they proved every bit as successful as on their home ground. From Padgate Junction a direct line to Sankey Junction avoided Warrington which was served by a loop through Central station. Padgate station would still hold unhappy memories for many for it was to there that many RAF conscripts travelled for their initial training at Padgate camp. (Eric Bruton)

The 0-6-0 wheel arrangement was widely used for shunting tanks, a frequently unsung species which nevertheless toiled away on menial yet essential work. The North Eastern Railway contributed the largest number of 0-6-0Ts to the LNER, the biggest class being the 119 J71s (NER Class E) built at Darlington between 1886 and 1895. Shunting engines they may have been, but they were still attractive in their proportions and were even favoured with brass safety valve covers, provided to encase the 'pop' safety valves after problems with escaping steam obscuring visibility. LNER No.8281 is waiting its turn outside Darlington Works where it had been constructed in 1892. Although some had vacuum brakes and steam heating to enable their use as carriage pilots, most (like No.8281) had steam brakes only.
(Author's collection)

A down pick-up goods approaches Hatfield, just north of Red Hall box, headed by a non-condensing N2/4 0-6-2T No.69590 on 16th April 1949, pottering along at about 20mph. The N2/4 version of this successful GNR class was introduced in 1928 but the evidence of this photograph is at odds with the authoritative RCTS history of LNER locomotives which states that all this batch were built with condensing gear and retained it throughout their careers. No.69590 clearly does not have it, yet it was an established feature of N2s working on the GN London area lines. The load is mostly empty mineral wagons, the leading one with a steel body, the rest of wooden-planked construction. An oddity in the train is a full brake, perhaps being worked away from Marshmoor yard after permanent way work in the area. (Eric Bruton)

Regarded by many as Gresley's finest design for the LNER, the V2 Class mixed traffic 2-6-2s performed outstanding work on the ECML. They dominated express freight work, taking over from the K3s, and could tackle any passenger trains with comfort except at the very highest speeds. This is a typical V2 duty — the down 'Scotch Goods' from King's Cross to Glasgow. On 22nd April 1950 a grubby No.60915 urges its fully-fitted Class C freight out of Hadley Wood North Tunnel, the train consisting mostly of vans and containers although at the front is a sheeted open wagon. The use of containers had increased throughout the LNER era despite their modest capacity and this method of freight handling can be seen as the forerunner of the later BR Freightliner operations and the most widespread type of rail freight haulage today. (Eric Bruton)

A southbound non-fitted express freight drifts steadily down the 1 in 200 gradient from Potters Bar Tunnel on 20th March 1951 in the charge of J20/1 0-6-0 No.64678. This was a Great Eastern design rebuilt by the LNER with round-top boilers from 1943 and the J20s' activities were largely confined to their home territory. However, No.64678 was one of four sent to Hornsey shed from 1951 to 1953 for working transfer goods to the Southern Region at Feltham. The load is certainly 'mixed' and includes a caravan on a low-loader, an early sign of a type of motoring holiday which was to grow in popularity. There are track workers on the down line, not exactly easy to spot in their dark clothing. (Eric Bruton)

Five North Eastern Railway 0-6-0 classes passed through *the LNER era and into State ownership. The J25s were introduced in 1898 (NER Class P1) but withdrawals had begun in 1933 and only 76 of the original 120 were still in service at nationalisation. Nevertheless it took until 1962 for them to disappear! Here we have No.65654, in a mixture of identity details, being coaled and watered at Springhead depot, Hull. Like many goods engines, it is not equipped with vacuum brakes. Note the loaded coal skips ready for tipping into tenders and bunkers; this was a full-time job for the shed coalmen, one of the steam age's least attractive occupations.* (Pendragon collection)

RIGHT:

York shed's J25 No.65656 comes smouldering out of Pickering on 31st January 1953 with a pick-up goods. The train is heading south past the engine shed and could be heading for Malton. On the other hand it could, bearing in mind the minimal load, be due to diverge west on to the Ryedale branch to Kirbymoorside on its last day of operation or east over the remaining stretch of the Forge Valley branch to Thornton Dale; the latter, however, was open only for stone traffic and the presence of a closed van in the very short train argues against it. (Pendragon collection)

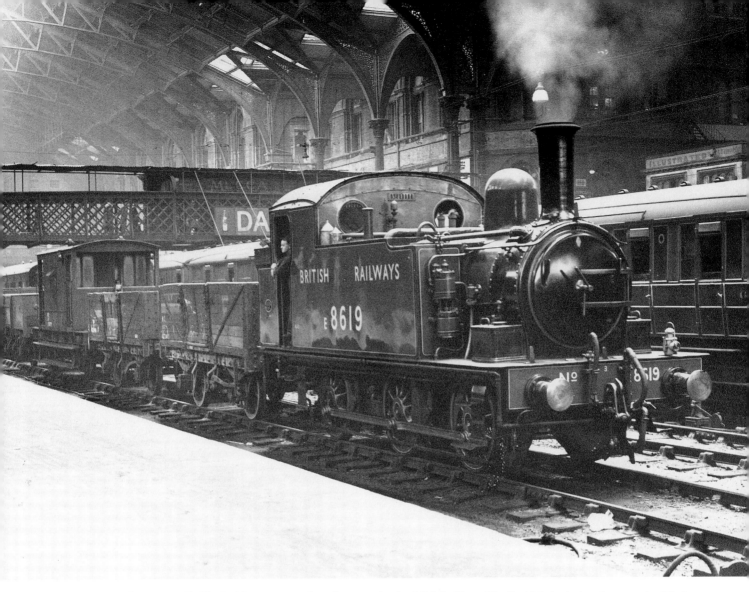

In January 1948 J69 0-6-0T No.8619 was appointed Liverpool Street station pilot for which role Stratford Works turned it out in LNER apple green livery but with British Railways markings and a temporary 'E' (for Eastern Region) prefix to its LNER number. The locomotive was immaculately kept, complete with burnished smokebox door rim and straps, buffers and pipework and clean oil bottles stored on top of the tank in front of the cab. On 24th August 1948 it was photographed on one of the sidings between Platforms 9 and 10 with a short train of wagons for removing rubbish from the station and the Great Eastern Hotel. These gallant little tanks (Classes J67 and J69) had originated in 1890 and began life hauling the busy Liverpool Street suburban services until relieved by the larger N7 0-6-2Ts during the 1920s, after which they were distributed around the LNER system fulfilling a useful role as shunting engines. Note the wartime covering over the footbridge still in place. (Eric Bruton)

Come the outbreak of war again in 1939 and the O4s were put on standby once more; 92 were called up in 1941 for service in the Middle East, 56 of which had already served with the ROD in France during the previous conflict! This time, though, they were not to return home. Even that was not the end of the O4s' military service as five were sold to the Government in 1952 for use at Suez! Edward Thompson's standardisation plans included a heavy goods 2-8-0 and the sheer quantity of O4s made them prime candidates for rebuilding to his design. Beginning in 1944, 58 O4s were given Thompson's B1-type boiler and cylinders with Walschaerts valve gear until BR terminated the programme in 1949. Meanwhile between 1944 and 1958 another 99 were less radically modernised with new Thompson boilers but retaining original cylinders and motion. BR did not finally dispense with the services of these admirable engines until 1966. An example is rightly preserved in the National Collection, though perhaps unfortunately the opportunity to acknowledge its ancestry has been lost by painting it BR plain black.

For the faster freights which the LNER introduced in the 1930s the company did not have a versatile 4-6-0 such as the

Slinking past Padgate signal box on 17th October 1953 is Great Central J10 0-6-0 No.65145 running light. This was another of the many long-lived 0-6-0 goods designs which lasted through LNER days well into the BR era, having first been produced by the Manchester, Sheffield & Lincolnshire Railway in 1892. Their continuing presence on the Cheshire Lines well beyond the London Midland Region's assumption of control after nationalisation was a reminder that the LNER had provided the motive power on the CLC. The stoutly-constructed wooden CLC signal box is worthy of a second glance, if only for the unusual steeple ventilator in the roof. The signalman seems to have been mopping the floor judging from the mops and buckets on balcony and the doormat draped over the handrail at the top of the stairs. There is no protective railing around the narrow balcony, just a handrail on the box itself in front of the windows — modern health and safety inspectors would not approve! (Eric Bruton)

GWR 'Halls' or the LMS 'Black Fives' but instead Gresley designed what many regard as his finest work — the three-cylinder 2-6-2 V2 Class. To build a large class (totalling 184 eventually) of sophisticated three-cylinder locomotives for fast freight and mixed traffic was very much an LNER approach but the contribution the V2s made, not just for their prodigious haulage feats during the war but on practically every sort of work on the LNER main lines, cannot be too highly praised. It can be argued that the V2s were perhaps the UK's most efficient steam type even if not the cheapest. The pioneer member of the class *Green Arrow* (taking its name from the railways' fast registered goods service) is preserved

In 1924 the LNER transferred the first of a number of Class K2 2-6-0s to Scotland and those allocated to Glasgow Eastfield and Fort William sheds could hardly have had a bigger contrast to the comparatively benevolent gradients of the GN routes than the mountainous West Highland line. The K2s in Scotland had to be versatile — passenger, goods and fish trains all came their way — but those used on the West Highland were rewarded by being named after lochs near the line in 1933/4. They also received improved cabs which offered more protection from the weather than the original spartan GN style.On 11th June 1951 No.61791 **Loch Laggan** *brings a brake van along the single line towards Fort William station, running alongside a public footpath which is separated from the railway by a fierce-looking spear-topped steel fence. The North British bracket signal carries the advance starter for the station box and a shunting arm for entry to the yards and motive power depot.* (Eric Bruton)

North British Railway J83 0-6-0T No.68477 rattles merrily towards Edinburgh Waverley station from Calton Hill Tunnel on 8th June 1951, below the remains of the old Calton Gaol and the later St. Andrew's House. These Holmes-designed tank engines worked assiduously and efficiently on local goods, transfer, station pilot and shunting work between 1900 and 1962. Unusually for the class, No.68477 is painted in fully-lined BR black livery with the owning name in full; only a handful of others received lined livery. In the background is a Thompson third class compartment coach. (Eric Bruton)

at the National Railway Museum though at the time of writing (2003) it is regrettably not displayed in LNER livery, surely the only appropriate one for a wholly LNER approach to motive power provision.

Yet Thompson did not favour the complicated derived motion of Gresley three-cylinder engines which demanded proper maintenance to keep it working effectively — maintenance which was not available during the war and in the years following. He preferred two cylinders or, for express passenger engines, three with independent sets of valve gear. Thompson made no move to rebuild the V2s but did produce the successful mixed traffic B1 4-6-0s which performed very much the same sort of work as the LMS Class 5s and GWR

'Halls' had been doing for some years, along with another useful mixed traffic class, the small-wheeled K1 2-6-0. The B1s entered production in 1942 and construction continued through the transitional years until 1952. The K1 type had originated with Thompson's rebuild of one of Gresley's three-cylinder K4 2-6-0s, a class of just six locomotives built in 1937-9 especially for the difficult West Highland line. No more were so treated but the prototype proved encouraging enough for a production run, with design modifications by Arthur Peppercorn who had by then succeeded Thompson, to be ordered by the LNER during its final year of existence. It was then left to British Railways to put the K1 Class into traffic during 1949-50, yet it was wholly a product of the post-Gresley LNER.

The pre-war goods train had often contained an eclectic mixture of privately-owned wagons, all bearing the markings of their owners, but wartime necessity had seen the wagons requisitioned by the Government for common useage. By the time BR came into being they were increasingly losing their old identities and the British Transport Commission subsequently purchased most of them, only for the railway operators to begin to dispose as quickly as they could of many of what they regarded as a poor stock of vehicles.

The bulk of the LNER's wagon stock was for mineral traffic and the company had perpetuated the old North Eastern Railway's practice of using high-capacity 20-ton wagons. Just

With steam to spare, K4 2-6-0 No.61994 **The Great Marquess** *(one of six powerful three-cylinder 2-6-0s built in 1937/8 especially for the West Highland) climbs the bank near Inverlochy with the 11.00am Class F non-fitted freight from Fort William to Glasgow on 19th June 1951, the leading vehicle being a six-wheel LNER van. On a warm early summer day the locomotive is working hard with a minimum of exhaust. The cloud-capped peak beyond the train is Stob Choire à Chearcaill, 2,527ft high, on the far side of Loch Linnhe.* (Eric Bruton)

The Woodhead route presented operational difficulties before its electrification. Express freights between Manchester and Sheffield were often entrusted to the K3 Class 2-6-0s; Gorton shed in Manchester had an allocation which was employed on express goods work to London, York and Lincoln along with the Grimsby fish traffic. Here is LNER No.1963 battling a strong cross-wind in the lonely Pennine moors near Torside in 1947.
(Pendragon Collection)

The Woodhead Tunnel problem is clearly illustrated in this view at its east end at Dunford Bridge with one of the admirable GCR-designed O4 2-8-0s No. 6276 emerging from the smoke-filled up single line bore. This photograph was taken before the war and, strictly speaking, is outside our period but is included to show the situation which drove the LNER to decide on electrification of the route. The tunnel was invariably full of smoke and the effects of the conditions prevailing inside caused serious deterioration of the lining, a state of affairs exacerbated by the increased volume of traffic during the war such that in 1946 the engineers had to take complete possession of both bores in succession for periods of nine months for essential remedial work. Faced with an ultimately insoluble problem, the LNER resolved in 1947 to construct a new double track tunnel. Note that a crossover has been laid and awaits installation of the final pointwork, part of which lies between the tracks. (Pendragon collection)

Living up to its mixed traffic reputation, B1 4-6-0 No. 61142 bursts dramatically from Hadley Wood North Tunnel with the down morning express fish van empties on 21st April 1951, fortuitously captured in a shaft of sunlight through drifting clouds. The leading vehicle is an insulated fish van of LNER design, with 15ft wheelbase and a through steam heating pipe to enable use in passenger trains if required. The deeply-recessed sliding doors indicate the thickness of the insulation slabs within the bodywork. BR built a further series in the late 1950s in the hope of winning back fish traffic already lost to road haulage. The train is running under Class C headcode for fully-fitted stock. (Eric Bruton)

over 250,875 wagons were passed to BR and the record of LNER wagon replacement had ensured that the average age of a wagon was about sixteen years, with only some 20% dating back to pre-group days. The trend towards speedier transit had seen about a fifth of the wagon fleet fitted with vacuum brakes by the close of the LNER period, but the nationalised era began with far too many unbraked wagons still running. These loose-coupled freights, lumbering along at slow speeds, were the bane of the railways for much too long and did nothing help them retain traffic in the face of the sharpening road competition that was to come.

An outstanding North Eastern Railway 0-6-0 design was its Class C, LNER Class J21, dating from 1886, which made up practically 10% of the whole NER stock at grouping. Although conceived as mineral engines, the majority received Westinghouse and later vacuum brakes which enabled them to earn quite a reputation for themselves on branch passenger trains, notably on the Stainmore route over the Pennines. The first withdrawal was in 1929, the last not until 1962. No.65042, pictured by the coaling stage at Heaton shed, Newcastle, was one of 171 constructed as compounds on the Worsdell-von Borries system. T.W. Worsdell, Locomotive Superintendent, was an advocate of compounding but his successor, his brother Wilson, was not and all the Cs were rebuilt as simples. After eighteen years as a compound No.65042 had been rebuilt as a simple in 1907 and ended its life with BR in 1954. (Author's collection)

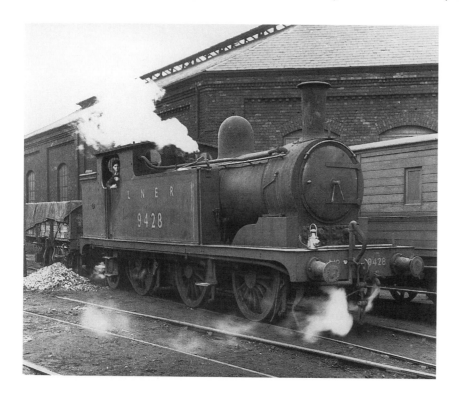

The NER invested in three classes of 0-6-2 goods tanks between 1886 and 1903, the first of which — from Thomas Worsdell — were mostly built as compounds, though later rebuilt as simples. These were followed by twenty simple expansion, but otherwise very similar, locomotives from Wilson Worsdell which became LNER Class N9. Heavy shunting, transfer freights and short-distance goods work were their forte although half the class of twenty received vacuum brakes which enabled occasional use on passenger trains. LNER No.9428 (location not recorded) received its new LNER number in 1946 but did not last long enough into BR days to be renumbered before its withdrawal in 1950. It is one of the vacuum-fitted examples but is also one of several equipped with carriage heating apparatus. Note the shunting pole on the front running board.
(Author's collection)

N7/3 0-6-2T No.69635 from Parkeston depot, Harwich, is working towards home as it approaches Forest Gate station with a short train of milk tankers in the early morning on 24th March 1951. On most lines it was rather unusual to see goods brakes working on milk trains, which ran under passenger stock conditions. No.69635 was constructed at Gorton by the LNER as an N7/1 in 1926 and was rebuilt with round-top boiler in 1944; these rebuilds were at first designated Class N7/3, changed in 1952 to N7/5 as a sub-group for LNER engines with short-travel valves. There is what looks like an overcoat streaming out of the cab. (Eric Bruton)

Moving the freight was by no means solely in the hands of the big heavy goods or mixed traffic locomotives and due acknowledgement should be made of the many shunting engines owned by the LNER, some of which were for specific local purposes. When in 1915 permission was granted for locomotives to replace horses in Aberdeen Docks, the Great North of Scotland Railway purchased four 0-4-2 tanks from Manning Wardle & Co. Two had 3ft 6in wheels and became LNER Class Z4, two slightly larger engines with 4ft wheels being Class Z5. All were allocated to Aberdeen's Kittybrewster shed and worked principally around the docks, with occasional short-term loans to private companies. Z4 No.68191 reposes in the noonday sun on the quayside. (Pendragon collection)

The Woodhead electrification is taking shape in this view near Mottram yard on 21st April 1951, with the overhead gantries in place. The motive power and train are, however, very traditional — an unkempt former ROD O4/3 2-8-0 No.63781 hauling wooden-bodied mineral wagons. No.63781, its identity barely discernible beneath the grime and limescale, was built for war service by the North British Locomotive Co. in 1918 and was amongst the first batch of surplus ROD engines purchased by the LNER in 1923. The ROD O4s were fitted only with a steam brake and never had any provision for working vacuum-braked trains. As part of the route modernisation the near track has been relaid with flat-bottomed rail and reballasted; the old chaired sleepers lie awaiting removal. (Pendragon collection)

GC O4/1 2-8-0 No.63799 heads a westbound freight between Penistone and Thurlstone on 30th June 1952, now running under the overhead wires. The electric haulage of freight trains between Wath and Dunford Bridge had been possible since that February but it would be another two years before the electrification of the Woodhead route was complete and steam could be banished. (Pendragon collection)

48

The NER entrusted its heavy freight haulage to 0-8-0s of which 215 were presented to the LNER. The total of 212 bequeathed to British Railways included fifteen of the mighty three-cylinder Q7 Class, the LNER having added ten more in 1924 to the North Eastern's original five. No.63466 blasts past Parkgate, just north of Darlington station, with a train of empty mineral wagons on 1st May 1948. It has been quick, for a goods engine, to be awarded its BR number but the 'NE' on the tender is the abbreviated wartime rendering of the LNER's identity. Externally, wartime neglect has merged into post-war neglect. (Rail Archive Stephenson/Photomatic 7970)

The LNER had felt it necessary to withdraw the passenger service on the branch from Melmerby to Masham, in the North Riding of Yorkshire, back in January 1931 but (as on many rural lines) goods trains continued to run for the benefit of the local communities. It sometimes seems these activities went almost unnoticed by higher authority, but the pick-up goods was still operating when BR took over and on 4th May 1949 NER A6 4-6-2T No.9791 had but two empty wagons to take from Ripon to Masham as it headed away from the main line junction at Melmerby. The Masham goods continued until November 1963 by which time a complaint had been voiced in the House of Commons that the branch was being kept open merely to deliver fresh water to the crossing gatehouses and coal for sale by the Masham station master (there still was one notwithstanding 30 years of closure to passengers!). (J.W. Hague/D.V. Beeken collection)

The North Eastern handed on 677 0-6-0s to the LNER, more than any of the other constituents, the last of which was the J27 (NER Class P3) introduced in 1902. These sturdy, hard-working 0-6-0s laboured dutifully on freights through the NE Area and in 1967 (along with the Q6 0-8-0s) became the last pre-grouping class to be withdrawn by British Railways. A filthy No. 5848 trundles northwards through York station on 2nd April 1949, passing an LMS 'Jubilee' 4-6-0 on a train for the Midlands or North West. York station has a look of post-war tiredness and is still controlled by semaphore signals before the signalling modernisation of 1951. (Pendragon collection)

The 2-6-4 wheel arrangement for tank locomotives became popular on the LMS and BR but its first manifestation came from the Great Central Railway with its twenty Class 1B engines introduced for goods traffic in 1914. However, coal output from the mines of Nottinghamshire and Derbyshire declined during and after World War I which, when combined with their lack of brake power, left the locomotives somewhat at a loss for suitable employment and their career eventually revolved around shunting and banking duties and short-distance goods work. The LNER classed them L1, then in 1945 L3 as their original classification was given to the new Thompson 2-6-4Ts. Neasden depot had an allocation which was used on local goods trips over the former Metropolitan line and here is No. 69064 out in the Chilterns near Wendover in the early 1950s before the L1s' departure from the London shed in 1953. (N.W. Sprinks/Author's collection)

The former NER J71 shunting tanks have already been mentioned but in 1898 Wilson Worsdell introduced a new 0-6-0T class (the E1) which had smaller wheels and larger cylinders. These became LNER Class J72 and a remarkably productive design it turned out to be. To the 75 the North Eastern had built the LNER added another ten in 1925 — constructed at the old Great Northern works at Doncaster! — and planned further orders, subsequently cancelled, in 1930 and 1931. That should have been that, for Thompson's standardisation plan favoured the GNR J50 type as the future shunting engine but under Peppercorn the J72 was included instead. A new order was planned for 1946 but was deferred until 1949 by which time it was left to British Railways to complete another fifteen, five more in 1950 and the last eight in 1951. Thus a design of pre-group origin spanned a total of 53 years in construction — under three successive owners! The J72s were certainly not confined to former North Eastern territory for a number went to serve in Scotland and examples could be found at various times at Ipswich, Wrexham and Bidston. In 1952 No.69014 went to St. Margaret's shed in Edinburgh where it was recorded alongside NBR J83 0-6-0T No.68448. Ultimately 49 of the class had vacuum brakes but not No.69014. (Author's collection)

LOCAL AND SUBURBAN

Whilst as far as passenger trains were concerned the LNER's public persona was very much focussed on the East Coast Main Line, at the close of its era it bequeathed to British Railways a network of 6,333 track miles (plus various jointly-owned routes of which more later). These ranged from important cross-country routes and busy suburban lines to a large number of rural branches which at best either teetered on the brink of viability or were sustained by seasonal traffic flows.

In Scotland there was, for example, the 'Waverley Route' between Edinburgh and Carlisle via Galashiels and Hawick which owed its significance as a through route to the Midland Railway's determination to secure itself a link of its own to Scotland; having striven to build its line from Settle to Carlisle, it arranged with the Glasgow & South Western

Railway to reach Glasgow and with the North British Railway to reach Edinburgh. The 'Waverley Route' was just as valuable, though, in providing railway communication with towns and small communities in the Borders and most of its trains were local in nature.

The LNER had a main line from Edinburgh to Glasgow but continuing north west of the latter it possessed one of the most scenic routes in Britain, the West Highland line to Fort William and Mallaig. This landed the LNER on the west coast of Scotland, certainly an anomaly in view of the company's name. However, in 1923 the grouping had taken railway companies in their entirety and placed them in the 'Big Four' without any real attempt to solve the issue of the so-called 'penetrating lines' which might have been more logically reallocated. Arguably the West Highland line should have

Class D11/2 'Improved Director' 4-4-0 No.62687 **Lord James of Douglas** *has just cleared North Queensferry Tunnel and is passing through the station there with the 2.30pm Crail—Glasgow Queen Street train routed via Thornton Junction and the Forth Bridge on 8th June 1951. The D11 is one of the Great Central class built by the LNER for use in Scotland and has gained BR lined black livery but the Gresley corridor coaches are still in teak. And where would a period station be without its Virol advertisements?* (Eric Bruton)

OPPOSITE PAGE
Apple green and British Railways for B1 4-6-0 No.61333 which has the obligatory oil lamps on top of the electric ones to denote the Class A headcode of its train. This is the up 9.27am 'Cambridge Buffet Car Express' (or 'Beer Train' as many knew it!) south of Hatfield on 16th April 1949. The electric lighting planned for the B1s was not the success that thad been hoped for. Some were fitted with alternator and all the wiring, some with just part of the equipment, some were built with none of it. The alternators proved troublesome so steam-operated generators were adopted but the system fell into disuse. (Eric Bruton)

been put in the LMS group which had the routes out to the west coast at Oban and Kyle of Lochalsh, but in 1948 they all found themselves together in the Scottish Region of British Railways. Nevertheless nationalisation saw little change for some time on this western outpost where LNER-designed 2-6-0s dominated, including the K4 Class of powerful three-cylinder engines produced by Gresley for this difficult line.

A vital cross-country route was that between Sheffield and Manchester, hewn through the bleak Pennines by one of the Great Central's ancestors, the Sheffield, Ashton-under-Lyne & Manchester Railway. The pivotal feature of the route was the Woodhead Tunnel whose original single bore of 1845 was duplicated by a second in 1852. The eastbound tunnel was on a rising gradient and the effects of years of locomotive exhausts pounding on the tunnel lining, combined with the smoky and often intolerable conditions inside, meant that this was a gruelling stretch of railway to operate.

In 1926 the LNER had decided that electrification was the best solution to to the operational problems of this route but the depression intervened. Ten years later the scheme was revived and work was to be assisted with the aid of Government grants to generate employment on major public works, but war brought it to a halt in 1939. Use of the original

The B12 4-6-0s came from the Great Eastern in 1911 as the company strove to provide more powerful locomotives which nevertheless remained within its strict axle load limitations. The LNER added another ten in 1928 but by 1931 the permanent way of the GE main lines had been improved to the extent that heavier locomotives could be accommodated and a programme was begun to rebuild the B12s with larger boilers. The LNER classed these as B12/3 and here we have No.61557 accelerating down Brentwood bank near Ingrave box after calling at Shenfield bound for Liverpool Street on 24th March 1951. Whilst the engine is regrettably grubby, the first two coaches have been recently painted in the new carmine and cream livery. (Eric Bruton)

single track tunnels was at first envisaged but such was their poor condition that instead the LNER resolved in 1947 to drive a new double track tunnel more suited to a busy modern railway. It was, however, the new Railway Executive which began the Woodhead Tunnel project in 1949 and pursued the electrification scheme to its completion in 1954.

In passing, it is worth mentioning that Woodhead was not the LNER's first brush with electrification. In 1904, to combat growing tramway competition, the North Eastern Railway had instituted a third rail 600V dc third rail system over a circular route between Newcastle, Tynemouth and Whitley Bay, one of the very first suburban electrifications in Britain (the first had been opened between Liverpool and Southport by the Lancashire & Yorkshire Railway only a week earlier). In 1938 the LNER extended the Tyneside system to South Shields and built 64 new twin-coach articulated electric units. For these it reverted to the old NER colour scheme of red and cream but early in the war decided that this bright livery made the trains too obvious a target for enemy bombers and from 1941 a more restrained Marlborough blue and grey was adopted. Following nationalisation BR began in 1949 to repaint the units in its standard green. The LNER also had a stake in the Manchester South Junction & Altrincham line, previously a joint GCR/LNWR operation and now jointly held with the LMS. In 1931 this was electrified on a 1,500V dc overhead system. Finally, two electrified oddities had fallen into LNER hands — the Cruden Bay Tramway, all 930 yards of it built by the

Great North of Scotland Railway in 1899 to serve its Cruden Bay Hotel but closed at the end of 1940, and the Grimsby & Immingham Tramway which the GCR had opened in 1912 and which actually lasted in BR ownership until 1961.

Although important secondary routes ran to such places as Hull, Scarborough, round the coast to Middlesbrough and Sunderland, across to Carlisle and down from Doncaster to East Anglia, the LNER had a substantial mileage of lightly-used rural branches which were never going to bring in much revenue — often anything but.

continued on page 58

Water cascades from the overflow of a full tender as B17/6 4-6-0 No.61652 **Darlington** *nears the end of Langley troughs with a Cambridge semi-fast on 3rd November 1951. Note the stone slabs laid over the ballast to prevent it being washed away by sudden deluges like this. The B17 is one of the 'Footballer' series of the 'Sandringham' class with the brass half-football under the nameplate and is as rebuilt with Thompson's standard B1-type boiler. 'LNER' is still discernible at the front of the leading coach which is thus still in teak nearly four years after nationalisation.* (Eric Bruton)

Secondary trains did not necessarily have secondary motive power! Blue-liveried A3 Pacific No.60105 **Victor Wild** *found itself employed on the 7.21pm King's Cross to Peterborough stopping train on 2nd August 1951, caught leaving Hadley Wood North Tunnel in the evening sunshine. The A3 is from 'Top Shed' and its excellent presentation suggests its use on a running-in turn after repairs. The carriages appear to be older Gresley teak stock relegated to secondary status for workings such as this.* (Eric Bruton)

In 1906 the Metropolitan Railway leased its line from Harrow South Junction to Aylesbury South Junction, including the Chesham branch, to the Metropolitan & Great Central Railways Joint Committee. From 1925 through Metropolitan trains changed from electric to steam traction at Rickmansworth and then in 1937 the LNER became responsible for providing the steam motive power. Former GCR C13 4-4-2T No.7420 trots along the Chesham branch with an auto train on 16th January 1949. These excellent tanks performed many years of local and suburban work over GC routes and No.7420 was one of two fitted in 1941 for the Chalfont—Chesham auto train service. The vehicles are some of the London Passenger Transport Board's oldest stock — ex-Metropolitan carriages built originally in 1898/90 for steam haulage, then converted to experimental electric multiple units and finally converted back for steam haulage. Two three-car sets were assembled for the benefit of Chesham branch passengers who had to wait until 1960 for London Transport electrification to arrive. (Pendragon collection)

LEFT LOWER:
In 1913 the North Eastern Railway had introduced a class of 4-4-4Ts for use on short-distance express passenger work but between 1931 and 1936 the LNER rebuilt them to the 4-6-2 wheel arrangement to make them more suitable for use on the steeply-graded lines of its NE Area. In this form they proved eminently suitable for the difficult route between Scarborough, Whitby, Saltburn and Middlesbrough over which they worked until the coming of diesel units and the demise of the coast line north of Whitby in 1958. LNER No.9881 runs along the cliffs above the North Sea at Sandsend with a Middlesbrough-bound train (including a fitted van at the front) during nationalisation's first summer.
(Ken Hoole Study Centre)

ABOVE:
N2/2 0-6-2T No.9533 marches its local passenger train through the outer suburbs north of Potters Bar on 26th March 1948. The train will be from King's Cross or Moorgate and the destination is not known on this occasion; the 'Cuffley' headboard is inverted on the smokebox door which suggests that the locomotive is on a filling-in turn between its rostered workings over the Hertford Loop. No.9533 is an LNER development by Gresley of his original Great Northern N2 design and is fitted with condensing gear for working through the tunnels of the Metropolitan Widened Lines. Apart from the engine being discouragingly dirty, nothing has changed following nationalisation. (Eric Bruton)

The Great North of Scotland Railway had relied to a large extent on a range of versatile 4-4-0s, as represented by LNER Class D41 No.6905 at Craigellachie with a Speyside train in May 1946. These locomotives (GNSR Classes S and T) formed the most numerous of the GNSR types. That company used the Westinghouse air brake but certain locomotives were vacuum-fitted for working through trains from the Highland and the LNER equipped the rest of the D41s with vacuum brakes. No.6905 did not enjoy a long BR career, being withdrawn in 1950. (Atlantic collection)

The former Great North of Scotland Railway system served a modestly-populated area of Aberdeenshire, Banffshire and Morayshire, with only its principal route from Aberdeen to Keith remaining today. In the Border Country branch lines ranged through the remote valleys of Northumberland, Roxburghshire and Berwickshire in an area between the Waverley Route, the East Coast Main Line and the Newcastle—Carlisle line. Thin pickings saw BR begin the closure of them in 1952, long before the shadow of Dr. Beeching fell across the railway scene.

Two trans-Pennine lines headed west to join the LMS — the epic Stainmore route over the tops from Barnard Castle to Appleby and Penrith, and the Wensleydale branch from Northallerton through relatively benign country to Hawes.

The latter's traffic was sparse enough to attract BR's cost-cutters in 1954.

The Yorkshire Moors and Wolds were full of branches. Whitby, for instance, was served by four lines of exceptional scenic attraction whose heavy holiday trade was to sustain them a while longer. In the post-war years passenger figures were particularly high and in 1947 the LNER opened a short branch from the Hull—Scarborough line to Filey Holiday Camp. However, Pickering was a country railway crossroads which was to lose two of its branches in early BR days — to Seamer on the Scarborough line in 1950 and via Helmsley to the ECML at Pilmoor in 1953.

Lincolnshire, Norfolk and Suffolk were also criss-crossed by branch lines serving largely rural areas. Closures had been undertaken by the LNER and continued during BR's early years; for example, the Wells—Heacham and Wickham Market—Framlingham branches were both deleted from the map in 1952.

A significant LNER presence in north west England arose from its participation in the Cheshire Lines Committee which had been formed in 1865 by the Great Northern and the Manchester, Sheffield & Lincolnshire (later Great Central) Railways; the Midland Railway joined the following year. After grouping the CLC continued jointly in the hands of the LNER and LMSR, the former having a two-thirds share and

The 3.35pm Hatfield—King's Cross makes the customary brisk getaway from Hadley Wood station behind Class N2/2 0-6-2T No.69493 on 4th March 1951, a photograph which nicely illustrates the articulated compartment stock — the infamous 'Quad-Arts' — which the LNER inflicted on its commuters. They have been repainted in BR red and would be around for quite a while yet; notions of 'the romance of railway travel' would probably be lost on GN suburban passengers. The station buildings are carried on the road bridge and the awning over the entrance is visible above the modestly decorative (for the GNR) cast iron parapet. To the right is a building which suggests itself as the station master's house. (Eric Bruton)

The North Eastern Railway G5 0-4-4Ts gave over 60 years' sterling service on local and suburban routes and the LNER fitted a number of them with push-pull gear. One such was No.67250, seen here not long after receiving its BR identity in October 1948 at Selby on a Goole push-pull train. Note the towering upper quadrant semaphores on the gantry, their height being dictated by the need to afford visibility to drivers through the station and above the bridge. Ascending to the highest arms to change the oil lamps is not a job for the faint-hearted! Also worth drawing attention to is the extended swan-neck water crane in the yard on the right.
(Pendragon Collection)

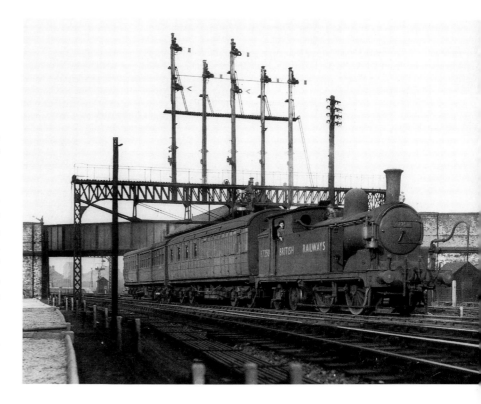

A transitional scene if ever there was one. K4 2-6-0 No.61995 Cameron of Lochiel takes the West Highland Extension at Mallaig Junction with the 10.25 stopping train from Fort William to Mallaig. Apple green engine, teak stock and only the fact that the K4 has gained its BR number mars the LNER illusion yet the date is 11th June 1951, 3½ years after nationalisation! Change sometimes came slowly to distant outposts! The K4, named after the chief of the Cameron clan, is one of six of Gresley's powerful three-cylinder 2-6-0s built specifically for the demanding West Highland line, a classic example of his 'horses for courses' traction policy. Behind its tender is a six-wheeled brake and luggage van, a common LNER feature carried on by BR. Towering over the bridge is a NBR Saxby & Farmer junction signal, the diverging arm 'off' for the train to take 'the road to the isles', arguably the most scenic line in Britain. (Eric Bruton)

providing most of the motive power. The CLC's most important route was between Manchester Central and Liverpool Central via Warrington and Irlam, offering the fastest service between the cities. There was also the busy link across Cheshire from Stockport to Altrincham and Chester, not to mention a branch off the Liverpool line across west Lancashire to Southport. The London Midland Region took on the Cheshire Lines after nationalisation but the LNER's influence persisted in the form of the motive power which remained at the local locomotive depots.

Historical legacy had certainly landed the LNER in some strange places in 1923. Its presence on the west coast of Scotland has already been mentioned but that was by no means the oddest, for the Great Central's bagging of the Wrexham, Mold & Connah's Quay Railway resulted in an

The LNER in Wales. This is Wrexham Central, end of the GC branch from Connah's Quay & Shotton where it met the Cambrian line from Ellesmere. In the bay platform, after arrival with the 2.00pm from Chester Northgate on 13th August 1950, is N5 0-6-2T No.69349 of Manchester, Sheffield & Lincolnshire Railway origin. The illogical 'penetrating lines' were never sorted out at the grouping and it was left to the Railway Executive to rearrange their post-nationalisation disposition. By the date of this photograph the GC lines in North Wales and the North West had been placed in the London Midland Region, though LNER motive power and stock lasted a good while longer. (T.J. Edgington)

LNER enclave in north east Wales and across the Wirral Peninsula. For good measure a branch of GC origin from the Liverpool line at Glazebrook deposited the LNER in Wigan and St. Helens in the very heart of industrial Lancashire, while a North British branch from Carlisle ran to an outpost on the Solway Firth at Silloth and a Great Northern branch straggled into Stafford. All these anomalies ended with nationalisation although not immediately, for the Eastern Region of BR at first found itself saddled with these 'penetrating lines' (the North Eastern Region in the case of the Silloth branch). However, on 30th November 1948 the Railway Executive announced a tidying-up of various geographical oddities nationwide and all these former LNER lines were more logically placed in the London Midland Region but, again, LNER motive power influence lingered. (As an aside, a further tidying of Regional boundaries in 1957 saw the North Eastern Region acquire various ex-LMS lines around Leeds and the West Riding.)

Whilst the generally impoverished nature of the LNER meant that it was unable to pursue the sort of 'scrap and build' policy which the LMS adopted towards re-equipping its motive power fleet, much of its pre-grouping inheritance was relatively up-to-date as compared with that of its rival and so continued to work on secondary routes and branch lines well into BR days. Gresley, furthermore, was not an adherent to the notion of locomotive standardisation, witness his 'horses for courses' approach to the provision of motive power. Relatively few new secondary locomotive classes were put into traffic but note should be made of the three-cylinder D49 Class 4-4-0s introduced in 1927 for 'intermediate' expresses in the North East and Scotland and the useful V1/V3 2-6-2 passenger tanks originating in 1930.

Thompson's modernisation plans of the early 1940s have already been mentioned and led, amongst other things, to the mixed traffic B1 4-6-0s and K1 2-6-0s which made an increasingly useful contribution in the hinterlands during the transitional years. In 1945 the first of a new standard LNER mixed traffic 2-6-4 tank appeared — the L1 Class — but the production build was set to work by BR from 1948-50. The L1s were employed in the London area, East Anglia and the North East and together the various new Thompson designs enabled some older engines to be withdrawn.

continued on page 67

This train carries 'express passenger' headlamps but it is debatable whether such an attribute can really be applied to the 5.30am Glasgow Queen Street to Fort William and Mallaig which, apart from omitting a couple of minor halts, stopped at every station on the West Highland line. Its Class A designation comes from the fact that the train conveyed sleeping cars from London King's Cross off the overnight 'Aberdonian'. A restaurant car was provided from Glasgow for the benefit of sleeping car passengers and other early starters; what could be better than to tuck into a full breakfast as the train pulled away from the Clyde and Gare Loch and traversed the magnificent mountain scenery? Eight coaches (all in crimson and cream) over this arduous route demanded two locomotives and on 19th June 1951 one of the now ubiquitous B1 4-6-0s No.61344 is piloting K2 2-6-0 No.61791 **Loch Laggan**, the former still having the 'BRITISH RAILWAYS' lettering it carried from new in 1949, the latter having progressed to the first BR emblem. Steam has been shut off as the engines drop down the bank towards Mallaig Junction on the approach to Fort William. (Eric Bruton)

LOWER RIGHT:

A rural railway curiosity in the north east was the North Sunderland Railway which ran between Chathill and Seahouses, in Northumberland. It was managed by the LNER from 1939 and then by BR until closure in 1951 but was never actually nationalised. In 1945 the railway hired a former North Eastern Railway 0-4-0 dock shunting tank,

LNER Y5 Class No.986 — BR No.68089, as its motive power and the locomotive was fitted with a vacuum brake and had the back of its cab filled in to give its crew some protection. Running under light railway speed restrictions, the North Sunderland branch train took twenty minutes to potter along its four miles. No.68089, practically overshadowed by its load of a four-wheel van and the railway's two ex-GER six-wheel coaches, jinks over the flat-bottom rails spiked directly to the sleepers c1949. (Author's collection)

Great Eastern route commuting in the days of the gallant N7 tanks, the 'Jazz' service and the notorious 'Quint-Art' articulated sets, two of which have been assembled to work this Liverpool Street-bound train passing Hackney Downs in 1948. No.9671 is one of the LNER's 1926 build of this outstanding GER design and still has the original Belpaire boiler; replacement of these by round-top boilers was under way and No.9671 received one in 1950. Condensing gear was original fitted to the class but was removed by the LNER in 1936/7 though the tank vent pipe in front of the cab was retained. The GER had been a user of the Westinghouse air brake and this system was retained on the N7s as it was better suited than the vacuum brake to the demands of closely-situated stations, quick stops and rapid departures.
(Pendragon collection)

LEFT:
This is how Shenfield line commuters travelled after the electrification was completed in 1949 and they were rescued from the 'Quint-Arts'. Three 1,500V dc three-car sets, ordered by the LNER but put into service by BR, are seen near Gidea Park on the 11.35am Shenfield—Liverpool Street on 5th October 1949. Ten years later work began to convert the units to 6.25/25kV ac following the decision to standardise on that system for the future and, as BR Class 306, the Shenfield units lasted until 1981.
(Locomotive Club of Great Britain/Ken Nunn collection 7815)

With the Lothian hills and the huge cantilevered girders of the Forth Bridge providing the backdrop, North British Railway 'Scott' D30/2 Class 4-4-0 No. 62429 **The Abbot** *draws into North Queensferry station with the 3.43pm Edinburgh Waverley—Ladybank train, composed of six different types of vehicle. The date is 8th June 1951 but the tender still has LNER initials. The starting signal on the opposite track has a bracket for a crossover to the down line for use when single track operation was in force across the bridge. On the right at the foot of the embankment is a steep path up from the bank of the Firth of Forth and the ferry landing stage.* (Eric Bruton)

In 1907 Wilson Worsdell of the North Eastern Railway produced his Class W 4-6-0Ts, ten powerful locomotives specifically for use on the gruelling gradients of the coast line between Scarborough, Whitby and Saltburn — the 'Whitby Willies', as they came to be known. Between 1914 and 1917 they were all improved by being rebuilt as 4-6-2Ts, giving them enlarged coal bunkers, and were then accorded the classification A6 by the LNER. The traffic over the Whitby coast line was extremely heavy during the summer months but during the rest of the year hardly merited the use of such large locomotives and they were later dispersed to depots where their power could be more gainfully employed. No. 69795 arrives at Hornsea on the 9.53am from Hull on 2nd August 1949.
(T.J. Edgington)

The Great North of Scotland Railway's Classes V and F were the final development of its 4-4-0s. The unsuperheated Class V was introduced by William Pickersgill in 1899 and thirteen were built up to 1911, though the impoverished GNSR had to let five of its intial order be sold by the manufacturers to the South Eastern & Chatham as it could not afford to pay for them. T.E. Haywood introduced the superheated Class F in 1920 and the two versions came together as LNER Class D40. A superheated variant No.62279 Glen Grant (all the GNSR F Class had been named) calls at Maud Junction with a Peterhead branch train.
(Pendragon collection)

In the rurality of East Anglia nothing much had changed in motive power terms during LNER days. Not many new types appeared to displace pre-grouping designs on country branches until closure or the advent of diesel units so there was still a strong Great Eastern atmosphere to the scene well into the BR period. One of the hard-working E4 Class 2-4-0s No.62781 (built in 1892) waits at Mildenhall as the 5.48pm to Cambridge loads its passengers on 18th April 1949.

(T.J. Edgington)

NER G5 0-4-4T No.67273 at Pickering on 1st August 1949 with a clerestory coach after working the 2.50pm from Scarborough via the Forge Valley branch. This lightly-used branch was to be an early BR casualty the following June. There are some nice platform-end details for modellers: water crane and tank and some NER slotted signals, one with a shunting arm, though the disc signal is of the LNER's upper quadrant type.
(T.J. Edgington)

The GCR Class 9N 4-6-2Ts were another example of a pre-grouping design to which Gresley added further locomotives when it was identified as being suitable to fill a particular need. The original engines, introduced in 1911, were for the Marylebone suburban routes but in 1925/6 another thirteen of what was now LNER Class A5 were built for the North Eastern Area. No.69820, at Immingham Dock on the 1.45pm from New Holland, is one of the last batch of GC locomotives delivered in the first year of the LNER. The date of the photograph is 3rd June 1952 by which time the GC A5s had mostly been dispersed from the London area. (T.J. Edgington)

66

A ramshackle byway with which the LNER found itself encumbered at the grouping was the Mid-Suffolk Light Railway which opened in 1904 between Haughley and Laxfield. Blithely disregarding the fact that no established railway company had hitherto wanted to venture across this sparsely-populated countryside, the Mid-Suffolk saw itself as a potential through route linking the Ipswich—Norwich main line at Haughley with the Ipswich—Beccles line at Halesworth, with branches to Westerfield and Needham Market for good measure. Neither the eastern link to Halesworth nor the branches were ever completed and the Mid-Suffolk remained an isolated branch in the middle of nowhere, existing in a parlous financial state. It does seem surprising that a passenger service survived into BR days; it took about an hour and a half to travel the nineteen miles of the branch which continued to run as a light railway, though the LNER finished replacement of the lightweight flat-bottom rails by the standard bullhead type in 1947. The curtain fell on this rustic outfit in July 1952, bringing an end to scenes like this recorded at Laxfield on 18th April 1949. GER J15 0-6-0 No.5459 and its pair of six-wheel carriages optimistically await custom with the 1.50pm to Haughley; someone has chalked 'LNER' on the tender, perhaps realising that nationalisation boded ill for the Mid-Suffolk branch. (T.J. Edgington)

The main lines out of London were, of course, host to local services of a totally different character to those found anywhere else on the LNER system. The GNR had inspired the expansion of the London suburbs out through the 'Northern Heights' along the main line to New Barnet, Potters Bar, Hatfield and Hitchin. To the railway fell the task of providing a regular suburban service which peaked at the early morning rush into London and the evening escape for home.

Electrification had been mooted by the GNR as early as 1903 and the LNER raised the idea again in 1931 with a proposal to electrify from King's Cross to Welwyn Garden City and Hertford North, along with the branches to Edgware, High Barnet and Alexandra Palace. There was, during the 1930s, the possibility of financial assistance from the Government but the extensions of the London Transport system out into the northern suburbs made the economics of the LNER's plans less attractive to the company board. The LNER branches to High Barnet and Mill Hill East were transferred to London Transport's Northern Line but it was to be the 1970s before the GN lines electrification came to pass.

On the Great Eastern busy suburban services were run to the populous districts to the east of London and into Essex. Again, the cost of electrification had been beyond the GE's means

The LNER D49 three-cylinder 4-4-0s were introduced in 1927 for secondary services in north east England and Scotland where the company wished to replace various ageing NER and NBR 4-4-0s. Here is No.E2773 **The South Durham** *with an up local at Baldersby, on the Thirsk to Melmerby branch, on 19th October 1948. It is of the D49/2 variant fitted with Lentz rotary-cam poppet valve gear which has its drive on the other side of the locomotive; all these were named after fox-hunts, while the D49/1s with conventional piston valves were named after counties. British Railways never regarded the D49s as important enough to gain its express passenger green livery and all were turned out in mixed traffic lined black. The Thirsk—Melmerby branch, linking the East Coast Main Line with the Leeds Northern route from Leeds to Northallerton, lasted until 1959.* (J.W. Hague/D.V. Beeken collection)

and instead it operated one of the most intensive steam-worked timetables to be found with the famous 'Jazz' services from Liverpool Street. The term 'Jazz' had become attached to these trains due to the bright colours applied to the carriages to distinguish different classes of accommodation.

As the LNER gave way to BR, London suburban services were still in the hands of indomitable 0-6-2T classes which had originated in pre-grouping days. On the GN line it was the N2 Class (dating from 1920) which held sway. Swift in acceleration and capable of a brisk turn of speed, the N2s were unchallenged until the diesels arrived in the later 1950s and the suburban footplatemen were masters of slick station work and quick turn-rounds in the terminus.

The GER had produced the N7 (LNER classification) in 1915 which was similarly unsurpassed on the suburban services from Liverpool Street. Electrification out as far as the rapidly-expanding areas of Ilford and Shenfield was proposed in the LNER's 1935-40 New Works Programme but work had only just got under way, with two miles of overhead line erected, before war brought matters to a stop. The project was resumed in 1946 and the electrification was completed to Shenfield by BR in 1949.

The LNER's provision of rolling stock for the GN and GE suburban services could hardly have been in greater contrast to its swish streamline and other main line trains. Suburban services were predominantly worked by trains of articulated compartment stock, a design which Gresley had introduced on the GNR. The LNER then built further trains of four-coach

N2/2 0-6-2T No.69521 guns out of Hadley Wood North Tunnel past Ganwick with the 2.59pm King's Cross— Hatfield 'all stations' on 20th March 1951, following the down afternoon express on what was then still a two-track bottleneck from Greenwood box. The N2 is one of the 'Top Shed' allocation and is reasonably clean. It was one of the right-hand drive GNR series built by the North British Locomotive Co. and carried condensing gear throughout its career. Its train is formed of two sets of 'Quad-Arts' — happy travelling! (Eric Bruton)

articulated sets — the 'quad-arts' — for GN services and five-coach sets — the 'quint-arts' —for GE services. They were, however, conceived not for passenger comfort but for packing as many people as possible into the least possible space (a concept by no means lost on modern designers!) and with compartment partitions only just over 5ft apart, travellers had to sit with knees more or less interlocked! The articulated suburban carriages continued through the transitional years to provide cramped and uncomfortable journeys for their long-suffering commuters and the last of the 'quad-arts' did not disappear from the GN line until 1966. The new electric units for the Shenfield line, ordered by the LNER before the war but deferred, were certainly modern by the standards of the time, with power-operated sliding doors, and their passengers would have found them far removed from the meagre and spartan accommodation they had for so long endured in the articulated stock.

B12/3 4-6-0 No.1516 charges up the bank from Shenfield to Ingrave with a stopping train to Liverpool Street in 1947. The LNER had resumed work on the delayed Shenfield electrification after the war and the overhead wires are in place, though it was to be BR which completed the scheme in 1949. The colour light signals on the down line replicate the indications of earlier semaphore signals.
(Pendragon collection)

Another look at the LNER's outpost in north east Wales, the result of the GCR's acquisition of the Wrexham, Mold & Connah's Quay Railway in 1904. Ex-MSLR N5 0-6-2T No.69281 calls at Connah's Quay & Shotton, in Flintshire, with the 3.50pm from Chester Northgate on 13th August 1950. (T.J. Edgington)

The LNER had running powers over a short distance of the West Coast Main Line between Penrith and Eden Valley Junction where the Stainmore line came in after crossing the Pennines from Darlington and Barnard Castle. On 14th June 1950 NER J21 0-6-0 No.65089 was photographed approaching the junction with the 9.30am 'all stations' to Darlington. The three coaches are all Thompson suburban stock from the close of the LNER period and all are still in the simulated teak finish. At either end there are two four-compartment brake thirds, offering a generous amount of brake van space for such a modest cross-country branch train. Between them is a semi-corridor lavatory composite; both first and third class sections have their own lavatory at the inner end of their short corridors, which change sides but are not inter-connected. As depicted, the corridor side of the two-compartment first is leading, then beyond is the white lavatory window and the compartment doors and windows of the third class section. (Eric Bruton)

The date is 16th June 1951 but snow still lingers in the corries as apple green-liveried K4 2-6-0 No.61995 Cameron of Locheil slows down for Banavie station and swing bridge where the line crosses the Caledonian Canal at the foot of a flight of locks known as 'Neptune's staircase'. The train is the 4.58pm Fort William to Mallaig 'express' in BR carmine and cream, a startling contrast to the residual LNER green of the engine; with a journey time of some 1½ hours for almost 42 miles during which it stopped at every station, the train's designation as an express is somewhat contradictory! A fine North British starting signal on a lattice post controls departure from Banavie in the up direction. (Eric Bruton)

The grandeur of the West Highland is summed up on the Horseshoe Curve near Tyndrum. In the evening sunshine of 9th June 1951 the 3.46pm from Glasgow Queen Street to Fort William, double-headed by a pair of K2 2-6-0s Nos.61764 Loch Arkaig (pilot) and 61770 (train engine), crosses the first of the two viaducts on the curve carrying the railway over the glens between Beinn Odhar, Beinn a Chaisteil and Beinn Dorain as it followed a course around their flanks. The grassy slopes of Beinn Odhar almost overwhelm the railway and the snow fence at the far end of the viaduct is a reminder that winters can be harsh in the West Highland mountains. No.61770 was one of ten K2s sent to Scotland in 1951 and still has its GN-style cut-away cab. The first two coaches are Gresley vehicles, the first still in teak and the second in the new red and cream. (Eric Bruton)

A grandiose railway scheme — and there were many! — was the Lancashire, Derbyshire & East Coast Railway which was planned to run from the Manchester Ship Canal at Warrington across to the Lincolnshire coast at Sutton-on-Sea where new docks would be established. As grandiose schemes go, it was particularly late on the scene, being incorporated in 1891; like many, however, it was only ever partially realised. The only length actually built was between Chesterfield and Lincoln and the Great Central took it over in 1907. British Railways was quick to dispose of passenger services between Chesterfield and Shirebrook North in 1951 and from there to Lincoln in 1955. C13 4-4-2T No.67427 has just arrived at Shirebrook North, an optimistically four-platformed station, with the 1.15pm from Lincoln on 11th December 1954. (T.J. Edgington)

Another passenger service to fall by the wayside quite early in the BR period was the Ryedale branch from a junction on the East Coast Main Line at Pilmoor to Coxwold, Gilling, Kirbymoorside and Pickering over which passenger trains ceased on the last day of January 1953. Sunbeck signal box was at the apex of a triangular junction of north and south curves from the ECML and its signalman has just received the single line token from the fireman of D49/2 4-4-0 No.62774 The Staintondale which is bringing the morning Pickering—York train off the branch on 15th April 1950. (J.W. Hague/D.V. Beeken collection)

*North Eastern Railway Class G5 0-4-4T No.67247 has steam
to spare as it heads a Sunderland local under the generous
roof of South Shields station. There is a couple of NER
clerestory carriages at the back of the train. Some rather
substantial iron railings run along the platform which is lit
by suspended gas lamps, below the bowls of which are horse-
shoe-shaped station nameplates. On the back wall, partially
concealed by a weighing machine, is one of the NER's
distinctive tiled maps of its system; these could be found at a
number of stations. One of the most significant features of
the scene, though, is the third rail electrification. To combat
growing tramway competition the NER had electrified its
suburban routes north of the Tyne in 1904, one of the
earliest schemes in Britain, and in 1938 the LNER extended
the electrification to South Shields. Note the NER shunting
signals situated precariously close to the live rails. The
blades of the crossover points stand so that neither lines up
with the running rails; they are moved separately according
to the direction required, for which the pair of shunting
discs act as splitting signals. Otherwise the switch blades act
as a form of trap points.* (Author's collection)

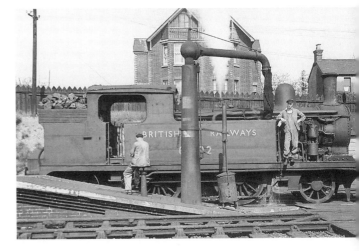

*No.67192, on its London suburban services. Many were
equipped with condensing gear for use when working in the
London area tunnels; No.67192 was given it by the LNER in
1923 and kept it until about 1954. As the larger engines took
over their duties, many of the 2-4-2Ts migrated to easier work
out of town; some even made their way to north east
Scotland and the North Eastern Area of England. As
No.67192 takes water at Witham on 17th April 1949, its crew
adopt characteristically nonchalant poses, the fireman lean-
ing on the tank, the driver perching on the water control
wheel.* (T.J. Edgington)

LOWER RIGHT:
*Before the coming of the more powerful 0-6-2Ts of LNER
Class N7, the Great Eastern Railway employed several
classes of 2-4-2 tanks, represented here by LNER F4 Class*

In the post-war holiday boom the LNER opened a short branch in 1946 from a triangular junction on the Hull—Scarborough line to serve the Butlin's holiday camp at Filey. Although open only during the summer season, Filey Holiday Camp station was generously furnished with four long platforms with run-round facilities, enabling it to accommodate the lengthy through trains which ran on Saturdays. Here, on a summer Saturday in 1947, cheerful holidaymakers step out towards the exit. The formality of dress — even when on holiday — is noticeable, particularly among the men; ties are worn by young and old. (NRM 292/82)

One of the Scottish D11/2 'Directors' No.62678 **Luckie Mucklebackit** *makes a steamy exit from the Mound Tunnel, surmounted by the National Gallery of Scotland, and proceeds through Princes Street Gardens with the 9.10am Edinburgh Waverley—Inverkeithing on 8th June 1951. Non-corridor stock, still teak-finished, but Class A headlamps — can this really justify being called an express?! The Scottish 'Directors' followed a North British Railway theme by being given names of characters in the works of Sir Walter Scott; in NBR style the names were hand-painted rather than applied as nameplates. Most of the Scottish D11s retained handle and wheel fastening of the smokebox door, whereas the English engines (D11/1) tended to receive the more familiar two-handle arrangement.* (Eric Bruton)

An up Royal Navy leave special is hustled through North Queensferry station by B1 4-6-0 No.61403 on 8th June 1951. The B1, one of the last batch of ten completed at Darlington the previous year, is fitted with extended lamp irons but without the associated electric headlamps. The smokebox numberplate was fitted towards the top of the door on the later engines which had their hinges spaced closer together. The first two vehicles are teak-bodied stock still in LNER condition; the third coach, emerging from North Queensferry Tunnel, is a door-to-each compartment vehicle repainted in red and cream. Modellers might like to try adding to their layouts the ramshackle collection of huts and corrugated fences in the allotments on the banking. (Eric Bruton)

NER J21 0-6-0 No.65103 stands on the turntable at Rothbury, terminus of one of the Border Country branches from Scotsgap. In fact, the branch actually ended on the turntable which gave access to the run-round loop, a small engine shed and other buildings which look like a goods shed of some sort and what is presumably a shed for a permanent way trolley. The branch passenger service did not survive beyond 1952 although excursions continued; the reporting number suggests that is what has brought No.65103 to Rothbury. (Pendragon collection)

One of the oddities with which the LNER found itself involved as a result of its joint ownership of the Cheshire Lines Committee was a branch off the Chester—Altrincham line at Cuddington to Winsford & Over. Its sparse passenger service dwindled away on the first day of 1931 but the branch remained open for goods traffic until 1958 and on 17th October 1953 an enthusiasts' special visited behind GCR C13 4-4-2T No.67436. The LNER's erstwhile motive power in the area was by then in the hands of BR's London Midland Region. Despite over twenty years of closure, the CLC station nameboard still stands, though the platform fencing is disintegrating. (T.J. Edgington)

BELOW:
The mixed traffic K1 2-6-0s arrived on the scene in 1949 via a prototype rebuilt in 1945 from a Gresley K4, a design modification by Peppercorn and an order placed during the LNER's final year. No.62030 has been elevated to express passenger duty in this early evening view on the ECML at Croft Spa on 10th June 1950. The reporting number and decidedly non-matching stock (the second carriage is of Great Central ancestry) suggest that this is an excursion returning to the North East.
(Rail Archive Stephenson/Photomatic 7109)

We end this section with a look at the blossoming of the LNER's plan for the modernisation of the Woodhead Route between Manchester and Sheffield. Work on the scheme had begun before the war but was then suspended; it was resumed afterwards but then came the discovery that the original twin tunnels at Woodhead had deteriorated to such an extent that the LNER was forced, in its final months, to decide on the construction of a brand-new double track tunnel. British Railways then took the scheme forward to completion with the formal opening of the tunnel by the Minister of Transport on 3rd June 1954. Two weeks later, on 18th June 1954, Class EM1 Bo-Bo No.26055 glides uneventfully out of the eastern end of the tunnel with the 4.00pm Manchester London Road—London Marylebone, the smoke and toil of the steam era consigned to history. The prototype of the EM1 electric locomotives was constructed in 1940, one of the last designs to appear during Sir Nigel Gresley's tenure of office as Chief Mechanical Engineer before his death the following year. A further link to the Gresley era is the LNER coach second in the train, still in teak finish and marring the modernity of a scene dominated by new tunnel, new locomotive and new BR MkI carriages. Who then could possibly have imagined the end of the Woodhead passenger service in 1970 and the abandonment of the route in 1981? (Eric Bruton)

RUNNING THE RAILWAY

The running of a railway is a complicated business involving a legion of workers pursuing a huge range of occupations, trades and professions, many on public view, many seldom seen, but all inter-dependent in one way or another. The average passenger or goods customer would think only of the train and its locomotive which would carry him to his destination or deliver and take away his merchandise. The only railway staff he might encounter would be at stations or goods depots or the guards and ticket inspectors on trains. He would certainly be aware of the engine driver and fireman, have glimpsed the signalman in his box and have noticed gangers on the track. However, there was, of course, a lot more to running a railway than the general public was aware of and to end this review of the LNER in transition here are some aspects of the work which kept the railway industry running.

Keeping the permanent way in good order has always been of fundamental importance — recent lessons have only served to remind us of that. There was no position of Chief Engineer on the LNER; the Areas had their own separate Chief Civil Engineers. It would probably have been the CCE of the North Eastern Area at York who planned this major relaying of the junction at Church Fenton, between Leeds and York, but when it took place on 17th October 1948 it was the CCE of the North Eastern Region of British Railways who was in charge. Several steam cranes are at work lifting and laying pre-assembled panels of track and pointwork which the large workforce of permanent way men would slew into position. Note the lack of any high-visibility clothing or hard hats in those days! (Pendragon collection)

Within LNER territory was a large number of racecourses and several areas where racing stables were situated, notably around Newmarket and in the North Riding of Yorkshire, so it is not surprising that the conveyance of racehorses was an important and often prestigious activity. The LNER provided a horse box hire service to carry horses between stables and station or station and racecourse. This photograph shows the LNER handling the removal of the Armstrong stables from Middleham (in Wensleydale) to Newmarket and was taken on 19th March 1946 at Leyburn station. The LNER handled the complete operation — road vehicles at either end and a special train for the journey. Horse boxes ran under coaching stock conditions and there would be accommodation for grooms; note the padding on the side of the stall to cushion the valuable animals during transit. No fewer than sixteen people are standing around to observe the loading of this horse ranging from railway staff, stable boys, someone who might be the trainer — and one lady! As road transport impoved, the movement by rail of all forms of livestock declined in BR days.
(Pendragon collection)

Permanent way standards on the main lines improved during the LNER era with the use of heavier rails and then flat-bottomed rails, now of course the standard. This official photograph was taken at Brayton, near Selby, in May 1945 to show the use of 110lb flat-bottom rail in a facing turnout. Note the track circuit wires joining the rails across the fishplates. Also worth a mention are the fogman's hut on the left in front of which is a '173' milepost measured from King's Cross, the two North Eastern Railway shunting signals on the right and the derailing ramp on the shunting neck which is laid in traditional bullhead rail. As a passing comment, all the photographs in this book show how tidy the track was — whether on main lines or branches, at stations or junctions — notwithstanding the wartime backlog of renewals and maintenance, a telling comparison with the weed-strewn formations seen all too often today. (Pendragon collection)

OPPOSITE PAGE

A range of battery-powered electric trolleys made the movement of parcels and passenger train merchandise around stations much easier and enabled 'trains' of trolleys to be made up which, under the control of a skilful operator, would snake along platforms, between passengers and around obstacles and corners. Here, at Scarborough Central station in April 1948, a battery truck towing three trolleys is about to disappear through one of those always intriguing 'Staff Only' doors but which is, in fact, the delivery access to the Parcels Office. The battery truck carries a range of boxes and packages which may well be railway material, along with what looks like a carriage window; one box has certainly not fared well in transit! At least one of the boxes is marked 'Smedley's', a name still recognised on tinned produce, and one package is stamped 'PEAS'. Following behind we have some office-type furniture, a bicycle, a trunk, some cardboard and wooden boxes, paper-and-string parcels, an LNER wicker basket probably containing laundry (there was a railway laundry at York), a mail sack and some milk churns. A glance around the advertising signs is often rewarding and reveals that Camp Coffee and Bovril are still with us, while Rose's Ales and Calvert's Disinfectant have disappeared. The Odeon was showing Singapore *starring Fred MacMurray and Ava Gardner plus a Laurel and Hardy film.* (Pendragon collection)

'Sandringham' 4-6-0 No.61646 Champion Lodge *strolls past Hatfield on 11th November 1951, the sun already low in the middle of an autumn afternoon, with a heavy-lifting crane (with relieving bogie and match wagon) after Sunday engineering work on a bridge further north. The locomotive carries a Class B headlamp code for "breakdown train not going to clear the line". Behind the crane is a venerable clerestory-roofed vehicle of GNR or East Coast Joint Stock origin acting as brake van and riding accommodation for the crane crew, but on this occasion the tool vans required for a breakdown train were apparently not required. The soaring semaphore signals, with their wooden platforms for intrepid lampmen, suggest possibilities for modellers; note the smoke shield under the gantry and also those below the bridge.* (Eric Bruton)

Among the railway workshops which the LNER passed on to the British Transport Commission was the important carriage works at York and a series of official photographs taken in September 1947 enables to look at some of the wide range of activities involved in carriage construction and repair.

Here we have two new Thompson carriages nearing completion in the erecting shop. They are steel-bodied vehicles but painted in the strange but effective teak finish intended to match them with the earlier teak-bodied Gresley era stock. Numbering and lettering has been applied though the carriages appear to be lacking their windows. The reasoning behind the pseudo-teak finish, which must have been time-consuming and costly to apply, is understandable but it looks odd on vehicles of considerably more modern outline than those of the previous generation. No doubt the LNER, in not opting for a new livery, was keen to avoid trains of mixed colour schemes — which was shortly to happen anyway in the transition to British Railways (and has continued to happen!). (LNER/Pendragon collection)

Remember when carriages had comfortable squashy seats?! The sprung seat cushions were stuffed with horsehair before being upholstered in moquette in the days before foam rubber filling. (LNER/Pendragon collection)

The fitting-out of carriages was largely in wood so there was plenty of work for the men of the polishing shop. Internal doors, tables and window frames are receiving attention, with lengths of beading stacked against the walls. There are carboys and bottles of varnish about, so there is probably quite an atmosphere in there! Extractor fans? Air-conditioning?
(LNER/Pendragon collection)

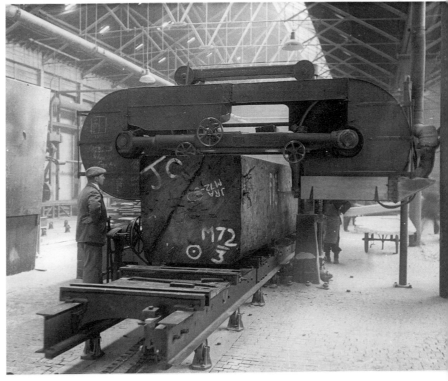

RIGHT:
This is how the wood started out in the carriage works. A five-ton log of figured mahogany passes through a huge band saw. (LNER/Pendragon collection)

Essential work, but well away from the supposedly glamorous railway jobs in the public gaze — filing journal brasses in the wheel shop. (LNER/Pendragon collection)

Equally as important was the work undertaken in the canteen kitchens to keep the hungry workforce sustained. A bank of enamelled ovens stands ready to produce a menu of the standard canteen fodder of the times. Various recipes are being concocted in mixing bowls and pans while in front of the battleship-style refridgerators, pastries are being assembled. (LNER/Pendragon collection)

The regulation of traffic and the sorting out of delays, breakdowns and other problems was in the hands of the District Control offices. This is the York District Control at 4.55pm on 27th July 1945 with the controllers keeping trains moving during the evening rush. A traditionally male world was infiltrated by women during the war and the lady nearest the camera has that essential item of railway equipment, a mug of tea. The York District Control was situated in what had once been the North Eastern Hotel, near the North Eastern Railway headquarters in Tanner Row, which the railway had acquired for office use in 1899. Later, BR's Regional Control was located in the former York & North Midland Railway boardroom in the offices at the original 1841 York station. (Pendragon collection)

Before the war the LNER had planned to modernise the signalling at York but the scheme was postponed in 1939. From the junction of the East Coast and Leeds lines at Chaloners Whin seven mechanical signal boxes controlled traffic through York, of which by far the largest was Locomotive Yard, at the south of the station. Dating from 1905, its 295-lever frame was the largest mechanical frame ever installed. This is the scene inside the box on 21st August 1948, with its frame stretching away into the distance. (BR/Author's collection)

The York resignalling project was resumed in 1946 and in 1951 a new power signal box was brought into use in stages by British Railways, being fully commissioned on 20th May. At the time it was the world's largest route relay interlocking system. This view of the power box, taken shortly after its opening, reveals a workplace totally different from the huge lever frames and block instrument bells of the seven manual boxes it replaced. The illuminated panel shows the extent of the layout controlled and 828 separate routes could be set with the switches. Above the panel are train describers which identified new trains entering the area controlled by the box. The number of signalmen was reduced from 70 to 27. (BR/Author's collection)